Sacred Then
and
Sacred Now

Sacred Then and Sacred Now

The Return of the Old Latin Mass

Thomas E. Woods, Jr.

Roman Catholic Books
P. O. Box 2286 • Fort Collins, CO 80522
BooksforCatholics.com

Copyright © 2008 Roman Catholic Books

All rights reserved. No part of this book may be reproduced in any form in whole or in part without the written permission of the publisher except for brief quotes in reviews or commentaries.

Printed in the United States of America

ISBN 978-0-9793540-2-1

Contents

Acknowledgments	vii
Note on Terminology	ix
1. Why Benedict Restored the Classical Liturgy	1
2. Benedict's Revolution	19
3. A Brief Guide to the Extraordinary Form	29
4. Important Features of the Extraordinary Form	55
5. Common Misconceptions	67
Appendix A: Pope Benedict XVI's Letter to Bishops, July 7, 2007	91
Appendix B: The *motu proprio Summorum Pontificum*	97
Appendix C: Useful Resources	105
Appendix D: Sermon of Father Calvin Goodwin, FSSP	109
About the Author	123

"What earlier generations held as sacred, remains sacred and great for us too, and cannot be all of a sudden entirely forbidden or even considered harmful. It behooves all of us to preserve the riches which have developed in the Church's faith and prayer, and to give them their proper place."

Pope Benedict XVI, July 2007

Acknowledgments

An author has debts to acknowledge even in a short book like this. The suggestions of Deborah Cole and Daniel Cole definitely improved my prose, and Kerri Lenartowick alerted me to important points I needed to clarify. Roger McCaffrey's reading of the text was indispensable; there is no one whose judgment I value more in such matters. My thanks to them all.

I am grateful also to *Crisis* editor Brian Saint-Paul, for allowing me to use in Chapter One a lengthy portion of an article I originally wrote for InsideCatholic.com, the web successor to the former print publication. A special word of thanks goes to Father Calvin Goodwin, FSSP, and to *The Latin Mass* magazine (for which I served as an editor for eleven years) for permitting me to use as Appendix D the excellent sermon he delivered on September 14, 2007, for the first televised Solemn High Mass in the extraordinary form in EWTN's history.

Finally, I would like to thank Heather, my wife, for her patience and understanding as her husband took on yet another project in his so-called spare time. This is it for a while, I promise.

Note on Terminology

With the publication of the *motu proprio Summorum Pontificum*, Pope Benedict XVI changed the very language we use to refer to the two missals in use in the Latin Rite. In the past, people were accustomed to speaking of the Roman liturgy that existed before the Second Vatican Council as the old Mass, the old rite, the Tridentine Mass, or the traditional Latin Mass. The liturgy promulgated after Vatican II, on the other hand, has been called the new Mass, the new rite, or the *Novus Ordo Missae*.

Pope Benedict XVI abandons this language (though *Novus Ordo* or *Novus Ordo Missae,* being the technical name of the new missal, is still acceptable). We are invited instead to conceive of these two missals as *two forms of a single Roman rite of Mass* rather than as two separate rites. The older liturgy is to be known as the "extraordinary form" of the Roman rite, while the new liturgy is to be called the "ordinary form." Other acceptable names for the extraordinary form include the Missal of 1962 and the Missal of Blessed John XXIII. (The Missal of 1962, in turn, is only a slight modification of the 1570 Missal of St. Pius V, which itself is traceable to much earlier liturgical books.) Likewise, other names for the ordinary form are the Missal of 1970 and the Missal of Paul VI.

These are the terms employed in this book.

Chapter 1

Why Benedict Restored the Classical Liturgy

By the second year of Pope Benedict XVI's pontificate, Catholic liturgy was all over the American (and international) media. The *New York Times*, the *Washington Post*, the *Los Angeles Times*, *U.S. News and World Report*—the subject was everywhere. The reason for all this attention was the Pope's long-awaited *motu proprio* that would liberate the liturgy of the pre-Vatican II Church (that is, the 1962 Missal), removing the legal restrictions that had previously limited its use.

This idea, once unthinkable in many circles, became mainstream practically overnight.

A blue-ribbon commission of prominent cardinals had concluded in 1986 that although Pope Paul VI had hoped that his new missal would supplant the old, no action officially suppressing the older missal was ever taken, and thus the 1962 Missal, even if largely eclipsed in practice, was never formally suppressed and continued to be a living part of the Church. The 1986 commission added that any priest ought to be free to choose which missal he wanted to use. Pope John Paul II looked at the question from the point of view of Church politics: with just about everyone in the hierarchy against such a move, he was fearful of taking so bold a step.

But the commission's finding is now the conventional

Sacred Then and Sacred Now

wisdom. Cardinal Darío Castrillón Hoyos, president of the Ecclesia Dei Commission and former prefect of the Congregation for the Clergy, Cardinal Jorge Medina Estévez, former prefect of the Congregation for Divine Worship, and now Pope Benedict XVI himself have declared that the Church's traditional liturgy was never abolished. In July 2007, Pope Benedict told the world's bishops that the 1962 Missal "was never juridically abrogated and, consequently, in principle, was always permitted." And with the Apostolic Letter *Summorum Pontificum*, issued *motu proprio* (of the Pope's own accord), freedom for the old liturgy—and not just the Mass but all the sacraments, and even the old Breviary—is now a fact of life in the Church.

The secular media, so often wrongheaded and hostile when it comes to the Church, was correct to sense that Pope Benedict's desire to bring back the traditional liturgy was something momentous. Still, some reporters managed to get the issue entirely wrong: some people want "Mass in English," they told readers, but others want "Mass in Latin." But the issue at stake has never been merely one of language. It is a question of two different liturgical books and two different ways of saying Mass.

Countless figures of prominence recognized what the Church was losing with the *de facto* suppression of the 1962 Missal. When nearly four decades ago it seemed as if the traditional liturgy would never be heard from again, a group of British intellectuals, Catholic and non-Catholic alike, issued a protest to the Pope that any such action would be a terrible offense against Europe's cultural patrimony. Signatories included Agatha Christie, Graham Greene, and Malcolm Muggeridge. It read, in part:

> If some senseless decree were to order the total or partial destruction of basilicas or cathedrals, then obviously it

Why Benedict Restored the Classical Liturgy

would be the educated—whatever their personal beliefs—who would rise up in horror to oppose such a possibility. Now the fact is that basilicas and cathedrals were built so as to celebrate a rite which, until a few months ago, constituted a living tradition. We are referring to the Roman Catholic Mass. Yet, according to the latest information in Rome, there is a plan to obliterate that Mass by the end of the current year....The rite in question, in its magnificent Latin text, has also inspired a host of priceless achievements in the arts—not only mystical works, but works by poets, philosophers, musicians, architects, painters and sculptors in all countries and epochs. Thus, it belongs to universal culture as well as to churchmen and formal Christians.

The petition concluded with a plea to the Pope: "The signatories of this appeal, which is entirely ecumenical and non-political, have been drawn from every branch of modern culture in Europe and elsewhere. They wish to call to the attention of the Holy See the appalling responsibility it would incur in the history of the human spirit were it to refuse to allow the traditional Mass to survive, even though this survival took place side by side with other liturgical forms."[1]

Pope Paul VI responded to the petition with an indult for England and Wales that retained the old rite as an option for special occasions. The old rite had won a tiny victory. More significant was what the petition itself seemed to show: even non-Catholics perceived something alienating—unjust, even—about the suppression of something as stupendous as the traditional Latin Mass.

That's where the matter stood until, in 1984, Pope John Paul II issued an indult allowing the 1962 Missal into the life of the Church once again on a very limited basis, and then broadened that allowance somewhat in 1988. The world's bishops often neglected the Pope's call to be "generous" toward those who favored the old liturgy. John Paul, who had

Sacred Then and Sacred Now

little interest in the matter, didn't push it.

But Benedict is very interested—so much so that he was willing to act even in the face of hostile or indifferent bishops.

In chapter two we'll look more closely at the Pope's 2007 liberation of the old liturgy. Here, though, we'll examine his writing on the liturgy while still Cardinal Joseph Ratzinger, in order better to understand the Pope's views and why he holds them.

Now it is possible to argue, as some indeed have, that the Church's liturgical problems are really only a secondary matter, and that it is more important to concentrate on the faithful transmission of the Church's teachings on faith and morals. But the liturgy is at the very heart of the Church—Vatican II describes the Eucharistic sacrifice as "the source and summit of the Christian life"[2]—and cannot be so neatly isolated from these other things. Our current pope, while Cardinal Ratzinger, argued that the crisis in the Church was closely related to the crisis in liturgy: "I am convinced," he wrote in his memoirs, "that the crisis in the Church that we are experiencing today is, to a large extent, due to the disintegration of the liturgy."[3]

Let us be clear: Cardinal Ratzinger did not regret that the liturgical reform ever took place. He declared himself pleased with the additional scriptural readings in the new missal, and the greater allowance for vernacular languages. Still less did he maintain that the new rite expressed the truths of the Catholic faith less precisely or explicitly than the old. In a 1983 letter to Archbishop Marcel Lefebvre he pointed to the new missal's retention of the venerable Roman Canon (now known more prosaically as "Eucharistic Prayer I") and its unambiguous references to the Eucharistic sacrifice to show that it was beyond theological reproach. (The Roman Canon was saved from the chopping block, though, only by the personal intervention of Pope Paul VI.)

Why Benedict Restored the Classical Liturgy

Ratzinger's unhappiness with the liturgical reform, therefore, did not include concerns about the doctrinal rectitude of the new missal. Those concerns were most clearly and consistently expressed by the late British author Michael Davies. Davies, along with the vast majority of traditionalist supporters of the old missal, never claimed that the Missal of 1970 did not truly confect the Eucharist. His complaint–expressed most systematically in his book *Pope Paul's New Mass*–was rather that it did not convey Catholic teaching, particularly on the nature of the ordained priesthood and the sacrificial aspect of the Mass, with the consistency and precision of the old.

It was not that anything heretical had been inserted into the new liturgy; what mattered, said Davies, was what had been suppressed. He argued that the changes to the missal did not seem random: their tendency was to remove or diminish prayers and gestures that highlighted these Catholic teachings. The new missal referred to the idea of sacrifice with language ambiguous enough to satisfy even some Protestants. Eucharistic Prayer II failed to include the word "victim," which in this context refers to Jesus Christ as the Divine Victim whose sacrifice on Calvary is made present on Catholic altars during the Mass. The indefectibility of the Church, argued Davies, meant that we could be sure that the Church would never fail in her mission, and thus the new rite was certainly valid. But it did not mean that she would always use the most effective or felicitous language to express her teaching.

It seems likely that these kinds of criticisms, even if not shared by Ratzinger himself, are not altogether forbidden to Catholics of good will. Following Davies' death in September 2004, Ratzinger wrote a moving eulogy to a man with whom he had enjoyed a good working relationship.

> I have been profoundly touched by the news of the death of Michael Davies. I had the good fortune to meet him

several times and I found him as a man of deep faith and ready to embrace suffering. Ever since the Council he put all his energy into the service of the Faith and left us important publications especially about the Sacred Liturgy. Even though he suffered from the Church in many ways in his time, he always truly remained a man of the Church. He knew that the Lord founded His Church on the rock of St. Peter and that the Faith can find its fullness and maturity only in union with the successor of St. Peter. Therefore we can be confident that the Lord opened wide for him the gates of heaven. We commend his soul to the Lord's mercy.[4]

What, then, *did* disturb Ratzinger about the liturgical reform? If he could not endorse traditionalists' critique in its entirety, he nevertheless shared some of their concerns. Ratzinger's writing on the liturgy consistently emphasized a number of key objections, some of which involved matters intrinsic to the reform and others that dealt merely with its unfortunate byproducts.

Before proceeding, one important note: some of the quotations that follow, which speak of mistakes and poor judgment in the liturgical reform that followed Vatican II, may make some readers uneasy or confused. But Pope Benedict weighs his words carefully. The problems of the liturgical reform that he has identified do not undermine the indefectibility of the Church in the least. Whether and to what extent the sacred liturgy should be changed are disciplinary matters and questions of prudential judgment, qualitatively different from binding statements of faith and morals. Only the latter involve the Church's claims of infallibility. For instance, a great many Catholic scholars have expressed displeasure with Pope Urban VIII's seventeenth-century breviary reform. Father Adrian Fortescue, an exemplary priest and possibly the greatest English-speaking liturgical scholar of the twentieth century, was unusually blunt: "No one who knows

Why Benedict Restored the Classical Liturgy

anything about the subject now doubts that the revision of Urban VIII was a ghastly mistake, for which there is not one single word of any kind to be said."[5] That summary assessment was severe, to be sure, but it was a criticism only of a disciplinary decision, not of a solemn proposition instructing us in faith or morals. And unlike infallible statements on faith and morals, such disciplinary decisions are subject to reversal—and Urban's breviary reform was in fact later reversed.

What, then, were Ratzinger's main criticisms?

First, he contended that the new missal gave rise to excessive creativity in liturgical celebration, which in turn undermined the very essence of liturgy and cut Catholics off not only from their past but even from the parish down the street, where Mass was celebrated differently. In *Feast of Faith*, Ratzinger wondered, "Today we might ask: Is there a Latin Rite at all any more? Certainly there is no awareness of it. To most people the liturgy seems to be rather something for the individual congregation to arrange. Core groups make up their own 'liturgies' from week to week, with an enthusiasm which is as amazing as it is misplaced."[6]

The Mass is not an evangelical tool to be radically revised from time to time in accordance with the sensibilities of the people. The instruction or edification of the people is not even its primary function. Its orientation, first and foremost, is toward God, not man. It is a solemn act of adoration and sacrifice that we are to receive in a spirit of docility from our ancestors, who have transmitted it to us down the centuries under the inspiration and guidance of the Holy Ghost. This is central to Ratzinger's critique: the very idea that liturgy is something to be *made* reflects a serious breakdown of liturgical consciousness. Ratzinger wrote: "Neither the apostles nor their successors 'made' a Christian liturgy; it grew organically as a result of the Christian reading of the Jewish inheritance,

Sacred Then and Sacred Now

fashioning its own form as it did so. In this process there was a filtering of the individual communities' experiences of prayer, within the basic proportions of the one Church, gradually developing into the distinctive forms of the major regional churches. In this sense liturgy *always* imposed an obligatory form on the individual congregation and the individual celebrant. It is a guarantee, testifying to the fact that something greater is taking place here than can be brought about by any individual community or group of people."[7]

There are those who complain that requiring strict fidelity to the rubrics infringes on the freedom of "faith communities" to devise the kinds of liturgies that suit them best. Ratzinger disagreed, and suggested that "the obligatory character of the essential parts of the liturgy also guarantees the *true freedom of the faithful*: it makes sure that they are not victims of something fabricated by any individual or group, that they are sharing in the same liturgy that binds the priest, the bishop and the pope. In the liturgy, we are all given the freedom to appropriate, in our own personal way, the mystery which addresses us." In fact, he turned the complaint around, noting that these manufactured liturgies themselves amount to a kind of tyranny exercised over hapless congregations, the vast bulk of which do not belong to parish liturgy committees. "Those able to draw up [manufactured] liturgies are necessarily few in number, with the result that what is 'freedom' for them means 'domination' as it affects others."[8]

On the one hand, Ratzinger argued, this was not the fault of the new missal. Speaking on the tenth anniversary of the *motu proprio Ecclesia Dei* (1988), Pope John Paul II's 1988 document on the 1962 Missal, he cautioned that "the freedom that the new *Ordo Missae* allows to be creative, has often gone too far." So far had it gone, he said, that there was often a greater difference between two celebrations of Mass according

Why Benedict Restored the Classical Liturgy

to the new missal than there was between properly celebrated offerings of the new and old missals.[9]

On the other hand, he implied that the new missal was not altogether blameless. "As concerns the Missal in current use, the first point, in my opinion, would be to reject the false creativity which is not a category of the Liturgy....In the new Missal we quite often find formulae such as: *sacerdos dicit sic vel simili modo* [the priest speaks thus or in words to this effect]...or, *Hic sacerdos potest dicere* [Here the priest may say]....These formulae of the Missal in fact give official sanction to creativity; the priest feels almost obliged to change the wording, to show that he is creative, that he is giving this Liturgy immediacy, making it present for his congregation; and with this false creativity, which transforms the Liturgy into a catechetical exercise for *this* congregation, the liturgical unity and the *ecclesiality* of the Liturgy [are] being destroyed. Therefore, it seems to me, it would be an important step towards reconciliation, simply if the Missal were freed from these areas of creativity, which do not correspond to the deepest level of reality, to the spirit, of the Liturgy."[10]

A second major theme in Ratzinger's corpus of liturgical writing is what he called *desacralization*. He told the Chilean bishops in 1988 that although many reasons could be cited to explain why a great many people "seek a refuge in the traditional liturgy," the primary one was that "they find the dignity of the sacred preserved there." After the Council, he explained, many priests "deliberately raised 'desacralization' to the level of a program." They argued that the New Testament had abolished the cult of the Temple, and that the tearing of the veil of the Temple from top to bottom upon Christ's death was meant to signify the end of the sacred. "The death of Jesus, outside the City walls, that is to say, in the public world, is now the true religion. Religion, if it has any being

Sacred Then and Sacred Now

at all, must have it in the nonsacredness of daily life.... Inspired by such reasoning, they put aside the sacred vestments; they have despoiled the churches as much as they could of that splendor which brings to mind the sacred; and they have reduced the liturgy to the language and the gestures of ordinary life, by means of greetings, common signs of friendship, and such things."[11]

A sure sign of desacralization, and the replacement of the sacred by a more familiar, man-centered ethos, is the reduction or even elimination of kneeling in liturgical settings. Ratzinger was a consistent opponent of the fanaticism against kneeling, and in his book *The Spirit of the Liturgy* recalled a revealing story from the sayings of the Desert Fathers. When God once compelled the devil to show himself to Abba Apollo, what was most striking about his hideous and emaciated frame was that he had no knees. "The inability to kneel," Ratzinger wrote, "is seen as the very essence of the diabolical."[12]

As we saw Ratzinger observe above–and as he has repeated again and again–the sheer variety and instability that characterizes the Missal of 1970 in actual practice, whereby the offering of Mass in one place can be quite different from how it is celebrated somewhere else, raises the question of whether there even exists a coherent Roman rite any longer. Yet for all this diversity, he said, there was one consistent feature on which the Mass-goer could confidently rely: they will be aesthetically dreadful. On *that* point these divergent celebrations of Mass do indeed resemble one another. "It is strange," Ratzinger once wrote, "that the postconciliar pluralism has created uniformity in one respect at least: it will not tolerate a high standard of expression."[13] And here again we encounter the phenomenon of desacralization, for how else are we to describe the substitution of 1970s banalities for the extraordinary range of Catholic musical patrimony?

Why Benedict Restored the Classical Liturgy

Ratzinger's third major criticism of the liturgical reform was that whatever its virtues, the new missal, both in particular sections and in its entirety, leaves the impression of a rupture with the past, and in some ways seems contrived. It resembles more a compilation by a committee of professors than the organic development of a truly living liturgy. "In the place of liturgy as the fruit of development came fabricated liturgy," Ratzinger wrote. "We abandoned the organic, living process of growth and development over centuries, and replaced it—as in a manufacturing process—with a fabrication, a banal on-the-spot product."[14]

Again Ratzinger faulted the new liturgical books themselves, not merely their clumsy implementation. "Even the official new books, which are excellent in many ways, occasionally show far too many signs of being drawn up by academics and reinforce the notion that a liturgical book can be 'made' like any other book."[15] The new missal "was published as if it were a book put together by professors, not a phase in a continual growth process. Such a thing never happened before. It is absolutely contrary to the laws of liturgical growth."[16]

Ratzinger cited the reform of the liturgical calendar as an example of "the armchair strategy of academics, drawing up things on paper which, in fact, would presuppose years of organic growth." This approach was "one of the weaknesses of the postconciliar liturgical reform." Those responsible, he said, simply "did not realize how much the various annual feasts had influenced Christian people's relation to time. In redistributing these established feasts throughout the year according to some historical arithmetic—inconsistently applied at that—they ignored a fundamental law of religious life."[17]

Ratzinger's claim that the organic development of the liturgy gave way in the liturgical reform to "fabricated liturgy" raises a more fundamental question, albeit one that he himself never confronted directly: does the Pope possess the

Sacred Then and Sacred Now

moral or even the legal right to make radical revisions to the Church's liturgy? There had been a great many changes to the Roman liturgy over the centuries, to be sure, but they had been gradual and organic, and typically imperceptible. There was never anything like what happened in 1969-70.

Cardinal Alfons Stickler, for one, has his doubts. Stickler, the retired prefect of the Vatican library and archives, was a *peritus* (expert) on Vatican II's liturgy commission. "I have never cast in doubt the dogmatic or juridical validity of the *Novus Ordo Missae*," Stickler recorded in his memoir. But "in the case of the juridical question serious doubts have come to me in view of my intensive work with the medieval canonists. They are of the unanimous opinion that the popes may change anything with the exception of what the Holy Scriptures prescribe or what concerns previously enacted doctrinal decisions of the highest level, and the *status ecclesiae*."[18]

Although the concept of the *status ecclesiae* defies perfectly clear definition, it refers to aspects of the Church's life "over which even the Pope has no right of disposal." According to Cardinal Stickler, there is good reason to believe that the liturgy itself "should belong to the *status ecclesiae*."[19]

Msgr. Klaus Gamber likewise doubted that the Pope had any such power. Gamber, an accomplished and respected liturgist, included a chapter called "Does the Pope Have the Authority to Change the Rite?" in his book *The Reform of the Roman Liturgy: Its Problems and Background*. (Available from Roman Catholic Books, Box 2286, Fort Collins, CO 80522; BooksForCatholics.com; $24.95.) "Since there is no document that specifically assigns to the Apostolic See the authority to change," he concluded, "let alone to abolish the traditional liturgical rite; and since, furthermore, it can be shown that not a single predecessor of Pope Paul VI has ever introduced major changes to the Roman liturgy, the assertion that

Why Benedict Restored the Classical Liturgy

the Holy See has the authority to change the liturgical rite would appear to be debatable, to say the least."[20]

Ratzinger wrote a laudatory preface to the French-language edition of *The Reform of the Roman Liturgy*, endorsing Msgr. Gamber's work and commending the author to readers worldwide. It must surely be licit to hold this opinion, therefore, for otherwise the cardinal would never have lent his name to an endorsement of such a book, or indeed such an author.

Although Ratzinger never actually addressed the question head on, it is perhaps suggestive that while *Sacrosanctum Concilium*, the Vatican II document on liturgy, says that no priest may change the liturgy on his own authority, the new Catechism, in the writing of which he himself played a great part, goes much further and says that even the supreme authority in the Church "may not change the liturgy arbitrarily, but only in the obedience of faith and with religious respect for the mystery of the liturgy."[21]

In *The Spirit of the Liturgy* Ratzinger came as close as he ever did to raising and answering this interesting canonical question. He will have no truck with those who take the view that the pope's authority is bound neither by tradition nor reason, and that his wishes and commands are *ipso facto* good and justifiable. "After the Second Vatican Council," Ratzinger writes, "the impression arose that the pope really could do anything in liturgical matters, especially if he were acting on the mandate of an ecumenical council. Eventually, the idea of the givenness of the liturgy, the fact that one cannot do with it what one will, faded from the public consciousness of the West. In fact the First Vatican Council had in no way defined the pope as an absolute monarch. On the contrary, it presented him as the guarantor of obedience to the revealed Word. The pope's authority is bound to the Tradition of faith, and that also applies to the liturgy. It is not 'manufactured' by the authorities. Even the pope can only be a humble servant of its lawful development and abiding integrity and identity."[22]

In light of these criticisms, it is not surprising that Ratzinger should have favored the wide availability of the 1962 Missal, since it pre-existed the abuses and problems that have accompanied the new missal. But it is important to recognize that he favored it not simply because he shared some of the concerns of traditionalists who were skeptical of the new liturgy, or as a grudging allowance to those stubborn souls who refused to get with the times—as the 2007 *motu proprio* was dishonestly spun even before its release. His support came instead from a deep personal love for the traditional liturgy, a love he shares with traditionalists.

In 2001 Ratzinger told a liturgical conference at France's Benedictine abbey of Fontgombault: "I well know the sensibilities of those faithful who love this [traditional] Liturgy—these are, to some extent, my own sensibilities."[23] On the tenth anniversary of *Ecclesia Dei* he expressed his delight at the fruits that John Paul's initiative had borne: "I think it is above all an occasion to show our gratitude and to give thanks. The diverse communities born thanks to this pontifical text have given to the Church a great number of vocations to the priesthood and to religious life."[24]

Ratzinger was also concerned that the Church's credibility was compromised by the idea that what was once her greatest and most cherished treasure could become forbidden overnight, and that a fondness for it could actually give rise to suspicion or derision. In the interview that became his book *Salt of the Earth*, he declared: "I am of the opinion, to be sure, that the old rite should be granted much more generously to all those who desire it. It's impossible to see what could be dangerous or unacceptable about that. A community is calling its very being into question when it suddenly

Why Benedict Restored the Classical Liturgy

declares that what until now was its holiest and highest possession is strictly forbidden and when it makes the longing for it seem downright indecent."[25]

The cardinal returned to this theme numerous times over the years. In Fontgombault he said that "in order to emphasize that there is no essential break, that there is continuity in the Church, which retains its identity, it seems to me indispensable to continue to offer the opportunity to celebrate according to the old Missal, as a sign of the enduring identity of the Church. This is for me the most basic reason: what was up until 1969 *the* Liturgy of the Church, for all of us the most holy thing there was, cannot become after 1969…the most unacceptable thing."[26] This, among other reasons, is why he "was from the beginning in favor of the freedom to continue using the old Missal."[27] "There is no doubt," Ratzinger said, "that a venerable rite such as the Roman rite in use up to 1969 is a rite of the Church, it belongs to the Church, is one of the treasures of the Church, and ought therefore to be preserved in the Church."[28]

As for *suppressing* the old Mass–which happened *de facto*, if not *de jure*–Ratzinger considered the idea not only pastorally unwise, but completely at odds with all previous liturgical history.

> It is good to recall in this regard what Cardinal Newman said when he observed that the Church, in her entire history, never once abolished or prohibited orthodox liturgical forms, something which would be entirely foreign to the Spirit of the Church. An orthodox liturgy, that is to say, a liturgy which expresses the true faith, is never a compilation made according to the pragmatic criteria of various ceremonies which one may put together in a positivist and arbitrary way–today like this and tomorrow like that. The orthodox forms of a rite are living realities, born out of a dialogue of love between the Church and

her Lord. They are the expressions of the life of the Church in which are condensed the faith, the prayer and the very life of generations, and in which are incarnated in a concrete form at once the action of God and the response of man.[29]

Liturgical rites can die out for a variety of reasons. The Church, moreover, "can define and limit the usage of rites in different historical circumstances." But "the Church never purely and simply prohibits them." And while Vatican II "did ordain a reform of the liturgical books," Ratzinger reminded listeners that it "did not forbid the previous books."[30]

These, then, are the reasons that Cardinal Joseph Ratzinger has been such a consistent advocate of freedom for the 1962 Missal. The details of Pope Benedict XVI's initiative on behalf of that liturgy—an act of justice, generosity, and common sense—is the subject of our next chapter.

---

1. The text of the petition is available at http://www.unavoce.org/news/2007/UK_Appeal_012907.htm.
2. *Lumen Gentium* 11.
3. Cardinal Joseph Ratzinger, *Milestones: Memoirs 1927-1977*, trans. Erasmo Leiva Merikakis (San Francisco: Ignatius Press, 1998), 148.
4. Leo Darroch, "A Very Unique Individual," at http://www.latin-mass-society.org/2005/michaeldavies.html
5. Quoted in Alcuin Reid, O. S. B., *The Organic Development of the Liturgy* (Farnborough, Hants [U.K.]: Saint Michael's Abbey Press, 2004), 38.
6. Cardinal Joseph Ratzinger, *The Feast of Faith: Approaches to a Theology of the Liturgy*, trans. Graham Harrison (San Francisco: Ignatius Press, 1986), 84-85.
7. Ibid., 67.

Why Benedict Restored the Classical Liturgy

8. Ibid., 68.
9. Cardinal Joseph Ratzinger, "Ten Years of the Motu Proprio Ecclesia Dei," Ergife Palace Hotel, Rome, October 24, 1998. Translated by Rev. Ignatius Harrison.
10. Alcuin Reid, ed., *Looking Again at the Question of the Liturgy with Cardinal Ratzinger: Proceedings of the July 2001 Fontgombault Liturgical Conference* (Farnborough, Hants [U.K.]: St. Augustine's Press, 2004), 150-51.
11. Cardinal Joseph Ratzinger, address to the bishops of Chile, June 13, 1988, available at http://www.unavoce.org/cardinal_ratzinger_chile.htm (accessed August 15, 2007).
12. Cardinal Joseph Ratzinger, *The Spirit of the Liturgy*, trans. John Saward (San Francisco: Ignatius Press, 2000), 193.
13. Ratzinger, *Feast of Faith*, 123.
14. From Cardinal Joseph Ratzinger's preface to the French-language edition of Klaus Gamber's book *The Reform of the Roman Liturgy*. Excerpts (including this one) appear on the back cover of Klaus Gamber, *The Reform of the Roman Liturgy: Its Problems and Background*, trans. Klaus D. Grimm (Fort Collins, Colo.: Foundation for Catholic Reform, 1993).
15. Ratzinger, *Feast of Faith*, 85.
16. Ibid., 86.
17. Ibid., 81-82.
18. Cardinal Alfons Stickler, "Recollections of a Vatican II Peritus," *The Latin Mass*, Winter 1999. Translated from the German by Thomas E. Woods, Jr.; the German essay appeared in Franz Breid, ed., *Die heilige Liturgie* (Steyr, Austria: Ennsthaler Verlag, 1997). My English translation is available online as of this writing at http://www.latinmassmagazine.com/vatican_ii_peritus.asp.
19. Ibid.
20. Gamber, *Reform of the Roman Liturgy*, 39.
21. *Catechism of the Catholic Church* § 1125.
22. Ratzinger, *Spirit of the Liturgy*, 165-66.
23. Reid, ed., *Looking Again at the Question of the Liturgy*, 152.
24. Ratzinger, "Ten Years of the Motu Proprio 'Ecclesia Dei.'"
25. Joseph Cardinal Ratzinger, *Salt of the Earth: The Church at the End of the Millennium*, trans. Adrian Walker (San Francisco: Ignatius Press, 1997), 176.
26. Reid, ed., *Looking Again at the Question of the Liturgy*, 149.
27. Ibid., 148.
28. Ibid., 149.
29. Ratzinger, "Ten Years of the Motu Proprio 'Ecclesia Dei.'"
30. Ibid.

Chapter 2

Benedict's Revolution

Pope Benedict XVI issued the *motu proprio Summorum Pontificum* on July 7, 2007. This was an extraordinary gesture, one of the handful of dramatic papal initiatives since Pope John XXIII called the Second Vatican Council. Those who for decades had worked and prayed that the Missal of 1962 be restored awoke to find their greatest hope finally come to pass. And they had also heard the Vicar of Christ say—contrary to what their critics had claimed for so many years—that it was neither wrong nor disloyal to have longed for the old liturgy. The Missal of 1962 was a great treasure that deserved its rightful place in the Church.

The Pope's point was so simple, so obvious, and yet, for nearly four decades, the laity had been all but forbidden to utter it in polite circles. According to Cardinal Darío Castrillón Hoyos, Benedict's gesture was "a Petrine provision emanated out of love for a great liturgical treasure, which is the Mass of Saint Pius V, and also out of a pastor's love for a considerable group of faithful."[1]

Not the least of what made this such a dramatic development was the indifference, even hostility, toward the 1962 Missal on the part of most of the world's bishops. That may seem strange: someone might *prefer* the new liturgy, but what

Sacred Then and Sacred Now

reason could there be for *hostility* toward the old, which generations of Catholics had found so beautiful and edifying? Indeed, Benedict failed to persuade the world's bishops to include even one line about the traditional Latin Mass in their synodal document on the Eucharist. Nevertheless, in July 2007 he went ahead with his initiative, convinced that resolving the Church's liturgical crisis was an essential ingredient in restoring the Church to health.

Summorum Pontificum was accompanied by an explanatory letter to the bishops. These documents, which appear here in Appendices A and B, deserve careful study.

In his letter, Benedict authoritatively confirms the canonical consensus we described in the previous chapter, according to which the traditional liturgy was never actually abolished. "This Missal," he writes, "was never juridically abrogated and, consequently, in principle, was always permitted."

Benedict contends that liturgical creativity undermines the mature liturgical sense that is supposed to inform Catholic piety. Many people wished to "recover the form of the sacred liturgy that was dear to them," he said, above all "because in many places celebrations were not faithful to the prescriptions of the new Missal, but the latter actually was understood as authorizing or even requiring creativity, which frequently led to deformations of the liturgy which were hard to bear. I am speaking from experience, since I too lived through that period with all its hopes and its confusion. And I have seen how arbitrary deformations of the liturgy caused deep pain to individuals totally rooted in the faith of the Church."

Benedict XVI makes a point of observing that young people derive great joy from the older missal. "It has clearly been demonstrated that young persons too have discovered this liturgical form, felt its attraction and found in it a form of encounter with the Mystery of the Most Holy Eucharist particularly suited to them."

An American cardinal who was (and is) unsympathetic to the traditional liturgy tried to claim during the 1990s that Pope John Paul II's allowance for it had been intended only for those who remembered that liturgy from their childhoods, and that with the passage of time there would be less and less "need" for such Masses. The Ecclesia Dei Commission, the pontifical commission that John Paul established to implement his *motu proprio Ecclesia Dei*, promptly corrected His Eminence, explaining that no such restrictions had been envisioned and that faithful of all ages were welcome to attend celebrations of Mass according to the 1962 Missal. With the issuance of Benedict's letter, the American cardinal's interpretation of the will of the Holy See was definitively excluded.

In his letter Benedict explains that the liturgical reform disrupted the unity of the Church, and suggests that Church authority (not for the first time in Church history) may bear some share of the blame for the persistence of those divisions. Here he surely has in mind the Society of St. Pius X, whose principal grievance was the de facto suppression of the 1962 Missal. "Looking back over the past," says Benedict, "to the divisions which in the course of the centuries have rent the Body of Christ, one continually has the impression that, at critical moments when divisions were coming about, not enough was done by the Church's leaders to maintain or regain reconciliation and unity. One has the impression that omissions on the part of the Church have had their share of blame for the fact that these divisions were able to harden. This glance at the past imposes an obligation on us today: to make every effort to enable all those who truly desire unity to remain in that unity or to attain it anew."

One of the benefits of making the old liturgy widely available again, therefore, is that it could bring about the reconcil-

Sacred Then and Sacred Now

iation of so many who currently worship outside the official precincts of the Church. And given that the Missal of 1962 is good in itself, and obviously in perfect harmony with the Catholic faith, why should we hesitate to grant it to those who so dearly love it? "Let us generously open our hearts and make room for everything that the faith itself allows," Benedict says.

Benedict then revisits a theme he highlighted with great frequency while Cardinal Joseph Ratzinger: the importance of continuity in Catholic liturgy. "In the history of the liturgy," he says, "there is growth and progress, but no rupture." Moreover, what was once treasured and prized cannot suddenly be despised and forgotten–the Catholic Church is not an Orwell novel. "What earlier generations held as sacred, remains sacred and great for us too, and it cannot be all of a sudden entirely forbidden or even considered harmful. It behooves all of us to preserve the riches which have developed in the Church's faith and prayer, and to give them their proper place."

And that is the purpose of *Summorum Pontificum*. No longer is the 1962 Missal to be attacked, ridiculed, or neglected. On the contrary, the Pope urges that "the Roman Missal promulgated by St. Pius V and reissued by Bl. John XXIII...must be given due honor for its venerable and ancient usage."

Now in addition to arguments from theology, philosophy, and ecclesiology, there is also a specific pastoral concern in Benedict's mind: those million or so faithful who have wandered from the Church's official diocesan structures, so great has been their alienation by the post-conciliar changes. It was Ratzinger who primarily brokered the agreement that would have reconciled Archbishop Marcel Lefebvre and his Society of St. Pius X (SSPX) in 1988, and he wept after the proposal collapsed. Benedict has had a sympathy for the SSPX over the years that has been understood by few and shared by fewer, even among his biggest supporters. Early in his pontificate Benedict held a private audience with Bishop Bernard Fellay, the SSPX superior general.

At the same time, it would be a mistake to suggest that the reconciliation of the SSPX was the sole motivating factor behind the Pope's *motu proprio*, or even the most important one. That is doubtless among the reasons that compelled Benedict's initiative, but it is surely not the most important one. Pope Benedict has many and varied concerns about the condition of the liturgy in the Church today, and he is likewise disturbed by the appearance of discontinuity in the Church's liturgical life. He has long wished for the Church to come to terms with her own liturgical tradition. The reintroduction of the old liturgy alongside the new makes that possible.

The freedom that this document allows for the 1962 liturgical books is sweeping. Religious communities who wish to use the 1962 Missal may do so, even exclusively. Priests may say their private Masses with this missal, and do not need the permission of their bishop or of the Holy See. They may also use the 1962 Roman Breviary.

Regarding the 1962 Missal's return to parish life, *Summorum Pontificum* explains that if a group of faithful wants this form of the Mass, pastors should accede to their wishes. "In parishes, where there is a stable group of faithful who adhere to the earlier liturgical tradition, the pastor should willingly accept their requests to celebrate the Mass according to the rite of the Roman Missal published in 1962.... Celebration in accordance with the Missal of Bl. John XXIII may take place on working days; while on Sundays and feast days one such celebration may also be held."

If the pastor does not satisfy their request, the people "should inform the diocesan bishop," who is "strongly requested to satisfy their wishes. If he cannot arrange for such

Sacred Then and Sacred Now

celebration to take place, the matter should be referred to the Pontifical Commission 'Ecclesia Dei.'" This Commission, established in 1988, will continue in existence and "will have the form, duties and norms that the Roman Pontiff wishes to assign it." It "will exercise the authority of the Holy See, supervising the observance and application of these dispositions." In other words, the Pope expects his instructions to be obeyed, and he has enhanced the status of the Ecclesia Dei Commission, which has the authority to enforce his will. His message to the bishops could scarcely be clearer.

In addition, the earlier liturgical books may be used for all the sacraments, not just for the Mass. Bishops are expressly given the right to celebrate the Sacrament of Confirmation according to the earlier Roman Pontifical, as indeed numerous bishops did in the years following *Ecclesia Dei*. And where there is sufficient interest, entire parishes may be erected in which all the sacraments would be celebrated with the 1962 liturgical books.

Just over a week after the release of the *motu proprio*, Catholic World News reported that Pope Benedict used the 1962 Missal for his private Masses.[2] It was an important sign that the days when it was acceptable to treat the pre-conciliar missal with contempt or indifference were finally over. The terms of debate in the Church had changed.

Although there had been little enthusiasm for the pre-conciliar missal before *Summorum Pontificum*, some favorable responses were indeed forthcoming once Pope Benedict's will was clear. The United States Conference of Catholic Bishops (USCCB) issued a useful and favorable series of questions and answers about Benedict XVI's document. Catholic News Service, an arm of the USCCB, promptly published an article directing the faithful to resources related to the old liturgy–missals, Latin pronunciation guides, videos, and training materials for priests.

Benedict's Revolution

Numerous American bishops, too, responded favorably to Benedict's call, and pledged to make more Masses available in the extraordinary form. "I am the only bishop in Wisconsin who does not now give permission for the Mass of Blessed John XXIII, as I did not feel the adequate catechesis was in place," said Madison Bishop Robert Morlino in the wake of the document. "But now that the Holy Father has indicated his desire for this extraordinary form to be more widely used, not only will the decree be implemented, but I intend to take the lead. I hope myself to celebrate this Mass, through which I found my own vocation."[3]

An especially helpful response, very much in the spirit of *Summorum Pontificum*, came from His Excellency William E. Lori, Bishop of Bridgeport, Connecticut. He recalled his boyhood days, when the traditional missal was in effect: "One of my prized possessions as a youth was the *Saint Andrew Daily Missal*, which contained Mass prayers in Latin and English, together with explanations of the rite. Following along with this Missal, my classmates and I had a clear understanding of the parts of the Mass together with their significance." Bishop Lori spoke with affection of his service as an altar boy: "My classmates and I took pride in learning [the] replies by heart and in achieving clear pronunciation of the Latin words. We were also fascinated by the intricacy of the Mass; under the tutelage of our assistant pastor, we learned to serve the High Mass and the Low Mass with effortless precision. Forty Hours, Confirmations, funerals, and weddings, as well as Holy Week (the rites for Holy Week had already undergone an initial revision) were special challenges which we relished."[4]

Bishop Lori went on to speak of "the enduring value of the extraordinary form of the Mass according to the Roman Missal of 1962. This Missal, though issued relatively recently, recapitulates centuries of liturgical development. In thinking

Sacred Then and Sacred Now

back to my own youthful experience of the liturgy, I am reminded not only of its antiquity but also of the formative role it played in the lives of almost everyone I knew, including my parents. The Mass and the Sacraments in this form nurtured the faith of great saints, Catholic intellectuals, and untold millions of ordinary Catholics."

By trying to re-establish the idea of liturgical continuity in the Church's life, said Bishop Lori, the Pope was helping to make the essential point that "you and I stand in communion, in a continuity of faith and prayer, with those who have gone before us. We are one with those who for centuries worshipped in liturgical forms which in the West gradually took shape until they were more or less standardized by Pope Pius V following the conclusion of the Council of Trent in 1563.... So with a mix of gentleness and firmness, the Holy Father is encouraging us to embrace all things Catholic in a spirit that seeks the unity and common [good] of the Church."

Embracing all things Catholic–that is precisely what Benedict's letter called upon the faithful to do. Bishop Michael J. Sheridan of the Diocese of Colorado Springs found it revealing that many of those who are so at pains to demonstrate their belief in "diversity" have been opposed to such diversity when it comes to the Church's traditional liturgy: "In a time when 'diversity' appears to be the newest virtue, it is just a bit ironic that some of the loudest protests against the Pope's apostolic letter are coming from those who have embraced every other kind of liturgical diversity–and anomaly."[5]

In the Archdiocese of St. Louis, Archbishop Raymond Burke promptly announced, in the spirit of *Summorum Pontificum*, "Courses of liturgical formation pertaining to the Roman Missal of Blessed Pope John XXIII will be provided for priests who desire it. The seminarians at Kenrick-Glennon

Benedict's Revolution

Seminary will be provided the liturgical formation necessary to celebrate the Mass according to the extraordinary form. Their studies of Latin will also give attention to the texts of the extraordinary form." Echoing Pope Benedict, Archbishop Burke also mentioned young people's attraction to the extraordinary form. "Not infrequently," he said, "I meet young people who are attracted to the former Order of the Mass, even though they had no experience of it when they were growing up."[6]

No one who was familiar with what Benedict had written on the liturgy over the past three decades could have been terribly surprised by this initiative or the rationales the Pope advanced on its behalf. The major themes we observed in Chapter One featured prominently in the *motu proprio* and the letter to bishops. Benedict's will is clear: the extraordinary form of the Roman rite is a great treasure of the Church, and should be actively fostered wherever there is a desire for it. The time for disparaging it, making foolish arguments against it, and treating it with contempt is over. What was sacred and great for us yesterday remains sacred and great for us today.

That's just common sense. And as of September 14, 2007, it is also the law of the Church.

---

1. Gianni Cardinale, "Nova et vetera: Interview with Cardinal Darío Castrillón Hoyos," *30 Days*, June/July 2007.
2. Catholic World News, "Pope Benedict Uses Older Ritual for His Private Mass," July 16, 2007, http://www.cwnews.com/news/viewstory.cfm?recnum=52403.
3. Fr. Raymond J. De Souza, "Why the Old Mass?" *National Catholic Register*, July 15-21, 2007.
4. The entire column is at http://www.bridgeportdiocese.com/column7.14.07.shtml.
5. Bishop Michael J. Sheridan, S.T.D., "Summorum Pontificum," *Colorado Catholic Herald*, August 10, 2007. Thanks to Daniel Cole for this quotation.
6. Archbishop Raymond L. Burke, "Be Not Afraid," *St. Louis Review*, July 20, 2007. Available online at http://www.stlouisreview.com/abpcolumn.php?abpid=13323 (accessed August 15, 2007).

Chapter 3

A Brief Guide to the Extraordinary Form

Since 1970, most Catholics have attended what is now known as the *ordinary form* of the Roman Rite of Mass. They recall the traditional Latin Mass, now called the *extraordinary form* of the Roman Rite, only dimly–or in the case of younger people, usually not at all. With the release of *Summorum Pontificum*, more and more Catholics will be attending the extraordinary form, so the purpose of this chapter is to help them navigate the old liturgy more successfully. Catholic authors have written a great many beautiful studies of the traditional liturgy and its inexhaustible treasures. This chapter, on the other hand, serves the more mundane but still important purpose of providing the beginner with a quick overview of the basics, and thereby making his experience with this liturgy easier and more fruitful.

If you are about to attend the extraordinary form for the first time, you will soon discover why Father Frederick Faber called it "the most beautiful thing this side of heaven." *Describing* the extraordinary form, on the other hand, is in some ways like explaining how to tie a pair of shoes. The steps sound confusing, but the action itself becomes second nature in no time at all.

Remember, above all, what the Mass is: the re-presentation

Sacred Then and Sacred Now

of Christ's sacrifice on Calvary. That one sacrifice is made present on our altars during Mass in an unbloody manner when the bread and wine are transformed in their substance into the Body and Blood of Christ. The separation of Christ's Blood from His Body represents His death. Every Mass we attend is as if we are on Calvary, intimately joining ourselves to Christ's Passion.

How would we comport ourselves if we really were at the foot of the Cross during Christ's suffering? We would probably not dress up in clown costumes or dance the polka—two phenomena that have profaned the Holy Sacrifice from time to time since the liturgical reform that followed Vatican II. We would instead be sober, solemn, and prayerful. That is just common sense.

And a beautiful solemnity is exactly what you will find in the extraordinary form. As Archbishop Raymond Burke of St. Louis observed, what attracts young people in particular to this form of the Mass is "the beauty and reverence, which the earlier form very much fosters."[1] That is what you are about to experience.

At the same time, the extraordinary form is more demanding of the worshiper. Parts of the Mass will be silent, as the priest says the prayers of the Mass in a low voice. The Catholic faithful must concentrate on the liturgical actions taking place, and pray the prayers of the Mass in the silence of their hearts. In the first televised Mass in the extraordinary form broadcast on EWTN, the global Catholic television and radio network, Father Calvin Goodwin put it this way. No one on earth has ever been more intimately united to the Passion of Christ than His Blessed Mother. And yet, as she stood at the foot of Calvary, what did she do? She made no outward gesture visible to the mortal eye. She uttered no words audible to the mortal ear. But her interior participation in the Sacrifice of Christ was more intense than that of anyone who ever lived, or ever will. And it is that kind of participation, in which our souls are united to

A Brief Guide to the Extraordinary Form

the actions of the altar, to which we must aspire. (The subject of "participation" in the liturgy is taken up in Chapter 5.)

First, some terminology. The Ordinary of the Mass is the fixed, unchanging part of the rite. The vast bulk of the liturgy, whether in the ordinary form or the extraordinary form, remains the same from day to day. The propers, on the other hand, are the prayers and scriptural readings that are specific to a particular day of the liturgical year. Hand missals for the laity typically include several colored ribbons for use as bookmarks, so that one of them can keep the correct page in the Ordinary while another holds the right page in the propers. So you will want to know which Sunday it is: the Fourth Sunday after Pentecost, for example, or the Second Sunday of Advent. You then simply turn to the correct propers for that day. The propers for the various days of the liturgical year will be in chronological order as they occur in the Church's calendar. If a special feast overrides the Mass that would otherwise be celebrated on that day, you can find the propers for that, too—normally in a special section of your missal dedicated to the propers for Church feasts.

One more set of terms: the Epistle side of the altar is the right side of the altar from the congregation's point of view, and the Gospel side is the left—so named because these are the positions of the altar from which the priest reads those portions of Scripture. It is said that the custom of delivering the Gospel from the left side of the altar developed early in Church history. The Epistle was understood as an instructive passage for the faithful, while the Gospel, which is ordered toward the conversion of the world, was to be proclaimed in the direction of the unbelieving world. With the priest offering the Holy Sacrifice toward the east, the left was the north side of the altar—which people associated with the pagan north still to be converted.

Sacred Then and Sacred Now

Finally, in what follows, P. indicates words spoken by the priest, and S. words spoken by the altar servers. The "dialogue Mass," one variant of the extraordinary form, allows the congregation to respond with the servers and recite or sing the ordinary parts of the Mass. The + sign indicates that the Sign of the Cross is made, either by the priest alone or by both the priest and people alike.

The traditional High Mass begins with the *Asperges* (or the *Vidi Aquam* during Paschaltide). The priest sprinkles the congregation with holy water as a portion of Psalm 50 is chanted.

> Thou shalt sprinkle me, O Lord, with hyssop, and I shall be cleansed; Thou shalt wash me, and I shall become whiter than snow.
>
> Have mercy on me, O God, according to Thy great mercy.
>
> P. Glory be to the Father, and to the Son, and to the Holy Ghost.
>
> [The priest and the servers pause for a moment and bow during the first part of the Glory Be, and rise for "sicut erat in principio..." ("as it was in the beginning...").]
>
> S. As it was in the beginning, is now, and ever shall be, world without end. Amen.
>
> Thou shalt sprinkle me, O Lord, with hyssop, and I shall be cleansed; Thou shalt wash me, and I shall become whiter than snow.

Thus the Mass begins with a moving reminder of the Catholic teaching on justification. The process by which our souls are made pleasing to God involves the washing away of our sins, in order that our souls might be made "whiter than snow." For Martin Luther, on the other hand, justification consists of the covering of our sins with Christ's righteousness, as with a cloak. The sins are not actually cleansed—which is why, in Luther's typically colorful language, he describes the justified man not as being whiter than snow, but as a "snow-covered dunghill."

A Brief Guide to the Extraordinary Form

Following the Asperges, the priest vests for Mass. He removes the cope, which is worn during the Asperges, and dons the chasuble. The people are seated while the priest vests.

The people stand as the vested priest approaches the tabernacle. He does not proceed directly but, wishing first to recollect himself, stops at the foot of the altar. He genuflects and then makes the Sign of the Cross. The people kneel. The priest prays the Judica me, a portion of Psalm 42. He reflects on his own unworthiness and seeks confidence and reassurance from God. "The altar is Mount Calvary and the Mass is the renewal, in an unbloody manner, of the Sacrifice of the Cross," a study of the spirituality of the Mass explains. "It is not difficult to see that the prayer of the priest at the foot of the altar resembles the Savior's last discourse in the upper room at Jerusalem and the agony in the Garden of Gethsemane. In those places [we encounter] the sadness of Christ at the beginning of His sacred passion; here the disquieted soul of the priest at the foot of the altar."[2]

But the priest summons his strength and courage, thanks to his trust in God. "Our help is in the name of the Lord, who made heaven and earth."[3] In a low voice, the priest and servers begin:

P. In the Name of the Father, + and of the Son, and of the Holy Ghost. Amen.

I will go in unto the Altar of God.

S. To God, Who giveth joy to my youth.

P. Judge me, O God, and distinguish my cause from the nation that is not holy: deliver me from the unjust and deceitful man.

S. For Thou, O God, art my strength: why hast Thou cast me off? and why do I go sorrowful whilst the enemy afflicteth me?

P. Send forth Thy light and Thy truth: they have led me and

Sacred Then and Sacred Now

> brought me unto Thy holy hill, and into Thy tabernacles.
>
> S. And I will go in unto the Altar of God: unto God, Who giveth joy to my youth.
>
> P. I will praise Thee upon the harp, O God, my God: why art thou sad, O my soul? and why dost thou disquiet me?
>
> S. Hope thou in God, for I will yet praise Him: Who is the salvation of my countenance, and my God.
>
> P. Glory be to the Father, and to the Son, and to the Holy Ghost.
>
> S. As it was in the beginning, is now, and ever shall be, world without end. Amen.
>
> P. I will go in unto the Altar of God.
>
> S. Unto God, Who giveth joy to my youth.
>
> P. Our help + is in the Name of the Lord.
>
> S. Who hath made heaven and earth.

The choir, meanwhile, sings the Introit, which is the first of the propers of the day's Mass. To follow the choir, the congregation may turn to the first page of that day's propers.

As the choir sings the Introit, the priest bows down and makes his confession of sins. The formula is somewhat different from that of the Missal of Paul VI–specific saints are invoked, and the *mea culpa* ("through my fault") is said three times instead of just once.

> P. I confess to Almighty God, to blessed Mary ever Virgin, to blessed Michael the Archangel, to blessed John the Baptist, to the holy Apostles Peter and Paul, to all the Saints, and to you, brethren, that I have sinned exceedingly, in thought, word and deed: through my fault, through my fault, through my most grievous fault [he strikes his breast three times]. Therefore I beseech blessed Mary ever Virgin, blessed Michael the Archangel, blessed John the Baptist, the holy Apostles Peter and Paul, all the Saints, and you, brethren, to pray to the Lord our God for me.

A Brief Guide to the Extraordinary Form

> S. May Almighty God have mercy upon you, forgive you your sins, and bring you to life everlasting.
>
> P. Amen.

The people and the servers now make their confession, which is said using the above formula with the exception that "you, brethren" is replaced by "you, Father." After the people make their confession, the priest says, "May Almighty God have mercy upon you, forgive you your sins and bring you to life everlasting." He then adds: "May the Almighty and merciful God grant us pardon, absolution, and remission of our sins." The congregants cross themselves at the word "pardon."

This exchange then follows:

> P. Thou wilt turn, O God, and bring us to life.
>
> S. And Thy people shall rejoice in Thee.
>
> P. Show us, O Lord, Thy mercy.
>
> S. And grant us Thy salvation.
>
> P. O Lord, hear my prayer.
>
> S. And let my cry come unto Thee.
>
> P. The Lord be with you.
>
> S. And with thy spirit.
>
> P. Let us pray.

The priest at last ascends the altar, praying in a low voice as he does so:

> Take away from us our iniquities, we entreat Thee, O Lord, that with pure minds we may worthily enter into the Holy of Holies. Through Christ our Lord. Amen.
>
> We beseech Thee, O Lord, by the merits of Thy Saints, whose relics are here [here he kisses the altar, in which at least one relic was traditionally contained] and of all the Saints, that Thou wilt deign to pardon me all my sins. Amen.

The priest now incenses the altar after having blessed the

Sacred Then and Sacred Now

incense (with the words, "Be blessed + by Him in whose honor thou art burnt. Amen"). The fragrance of the incense symbolizes our desire to purify and sanctify ourselves as we worship God. That the incense is something burned suggests the burning zeal that should animate the souls of the faithful. The smoke also represents the prayers of the faithful ascending to heaven.

When he is finished incensing the altar, the priest proceeds to the Epistle side to chant the Introit, as the choir begins to sing the Kyrie. Returning to the center of the altar he prays the Kyrie (which is also found, in abbreviated form, in the new missal).

> P. Lord, have mercy.
>
> S. Lord, have mercy.
>
> P. Lord, have mercy.
>
> S. Christ, have mercy.
>
> P. Christ, have mercy.
>
> S. Christ, have mercy.
>
> P. Lord, have mercy.
>
> S. Lord, have mercy.
>
> P. Lord, have mercy.

As in the new missal, the Kyrie is followed by the Gloria. All stand when the priest intones, "Gloria in excelsis Deo."

> Glory be to God on high. And on earth peace to men of good will. We praise Thee. We bless Thee. We adore Thee. We glorify Thee. We give Thee thanks for Thy great glory. Lord God, heavenly King, God the Father Almighty. Lord Jesus Christ, Only-begotten Son, Lord God, Lamb of God, Son of the Father. Thou Who takest away the sins of the world, have mercy on us. Thou who takest away the sins of the world, receive our prayer. Thou Who sittest at the right hand of the Father, have mercy on us. For Thou alone art holy. Thou alone, O

A Brief Guide to the Extraordinary Form

Jesus Christ, art most high. With the Holy Ghost, + in the glory of God the Father. Amen.

As the choir continues the Gloria following the priest's initial intonation, the priest recites the remainder in a low voice. Since the prayer is spoken more rapidly than it is chanted, the priest will finish the Gloria before the choir and people. When he finishes, he genuflects and is seated at the Epistle side. All in the congregation are seated when the priest is seated, even though the Gloria is still being sung. Note during the singing of the Gloria that the priest bows his head at each of the two mentions of Christ's name. As the Gloria nears its end, the priest rises and proceeds to the altar–at which point the people themselves rise once again and, in a dialogue Mass, respond "Et cum spiritu tuo" ("And with thy spirit") to the priest's "Dominus vobiscum" ("The Lord be with you").

After the Gloria the priest prays the Collect, which is another of the propers. Various explanations for the name of this prayer have been advanced. The simplest comes from Pope Innocent III, who said that the priest here *collects* together the prayers of all the people.[4]

The Collect, in turn, is followed by the Epistle, during which the people are seated–the traditional posture for receiving instruction. The Epistle for the day is found in the missal among the propers. After the Epistle come two other prayers, the Gradual and an Alleluia (except during penitential seasons, when the latter is replaced by a psalm or excerpt thereof called a Tract).

After the Alleluia one of the servers transfers the altar missal from the Epistle side to the Gospel side. The people rise as the priest says "Dominus vobiscum" and cross themselves on the forehead, lips, and heart, just as in the ordinary form, since the priest is about to read the Gospel. Just before reading it he prays the Munda Cor Meum:

Sacred Then and Sacred Now

> Cleanse my heart and my lips, O Almighty God, Who didst cleanse the lips of the prophet Isaias with a burning coal; through Thy gracious mercy so purify me that I may worthily proclaim Thy holy Gospel. Through Christ our Lord. Amen.

At the conclusion of the Gospel the priest prays silently, "By the words of the Gospel may our sins be blotted out."

It is now time for the sermon, or homily. Proceeding to the pulpit, the priest typically reads the Epistle and the Gospel in the vernacular for the people. After perhaps making a few announcements, he makes the Sign of the Cross and begins the sermon, which likewise concludes with the Sign of the Cross.

There is no pause for meditation following the sermon. The priest and servers proceed directly to the altar for the Creed. As with the Gloria, the priest intones the opening words–in this case, "Credo in unum Deum." The choir and the people then continue to sing, as the priest silently recites the rest of the Creed.

> I believe in one God, the Father Almighty, Maker of heaven and earth, and of all things visible and invisible. And in one Lord Jesus Christ, the Only-begotten Son of God. Born of the Father before all ages. God of God, Light of Light, true God of true God. Begotten, not made, consubstantial with the Father, by Whom all things were made. Who for us men, and for our salvation, came down from heaven.
>
> [All kneel.]
>
> And was incarnate by the Holy Ghost of the Virgin Mary: and was made man.
>
> [All stand.]
>
> He was crucified also for us, suffered under Pontius Pilate, and was buried. And on the third day He rose again according to the Scriptures. And He ascended into heaven, and sitteth at the right hand of the Father. And

A Brief Guide to the Extraordinary Form

He shall come again with glory to judge the living and the dead: of Whose kingdom there shall be no end.

And in the Holy Ghost, the Lord and Giver of Life: Who proceedeth from the Father and the Son. Who together with the Father and the Son is adored and glorified, Who spoke through the Prophets. And in One, Holy, Catholic and Apostolic Church. I confess one Baptism for the remission of sins. And I look for the resurrection of the dead, and the life + of the world to come. Amen.

Since the priest is praying the Creed at a different pace from that of the choir and the people (he is speaking in a low voice and they are singing), he will likely reach the point at which kneeling is called for (at the words "*Et incarnatus est de Spiritu Sancto ex Maria Virgine, et homo factus est*") before the people do. *The people do not kneel at this time.* They continue singing the Creed, and kneel when *they* reach the reference to Christ's Incarnation.

When the priest finishes reciting the Creed he is seated at the Epistle side of the altar. When the priest is seated, the people also sit for the remainder of the Creed and rise again toward the end in tandem with the priest, who now returns to the altar.

Following another "Dominus vobiscum" exchange, we now reach the Offertory (known in the Missal of Paul VI as the Preparation of the Gifts). First the priest recites the Offertory antiphon, a proper. Observe in the prayers that then follow that the priest speaks of the unconsecrated bread and wine as if they have already been consecrated. He is speaking *by anticipation*, and thinking of what the bread and wine will become in just a few short moments. This practice is also observed in the venerable Eastern rites of the Catholic Church.

Consider this striking prayer:

Accept, O Holy father, Almighty and Eternal God, this spotless host, which I, Your unworthy servant, offer to You, my living and true God, to atone for my numberless

Sacred Then and Sacred Now

> sins, offences, and negligences; on behalf of all here present and likewise for all faithful Christians living and dead, that it may profit me and them as a means of salvation to life everlasting. Amen.
>
> We offer unto Thee, O Lord, the chalice of salvation, entreating Thy mercy that our offering may ascend with a sweet fragrance in the sight of Thy divine Majesty, for our own salvation, and for that of the whole world. Amen.
>
> Humbled in spirit and contrite of heart, may we find favor with Thee, O Lord: and may our sacrifice be so offered this day in Thy sight as to be pleasing to Thee, O Lord God.
>
> Come Thou, the Sanctifier, Almighty and Everlasting God, and bless + this sacrifice which is prepared for the glory of Thy holy Name.

Some modern liturgists have been hostile to the Offertory prayers in the 1962 Missal for precisely this reason: why should the unconsecrated bread and wine be treated as if already consecrated? Surely this is some kind of error that needs to be excised. But Monsignor Ronald Knox showed why this classical usage makes good sense:

> It's all very well for you to point out that the Offertory is only concerned with unconsecrated bread and wine, and that isn't much to get excited about. That's quite true, of course, but I think if you will use your imagination for a moment you will see that there is good excuse for making a lot of the unconsecrated host, the unconsecrated chalice. They may have no importance of their own at the moment, but they are *going* to be terrifically important. And it's very narrow-minded of us if we think only of what things are at the moment, not of what they are going to be.

Imagine walking through a field of wheat, Msgr. Knox proposed. Each ear of that wheat is destined to become something. One will become part of a sandwich that someone will eat on a railway journey. But another will (after being threshed, ground in the mill, and baked) be "pressed by a Carmelite nun in a press which will give it the imprint of the crucifix; it will be sent off in a tin to the sacristan of some church; it will lie on the altar, some Latin words will be said over it, and after that it will be lifted up in a gold monstrance, and everybody who passes in front of it will go down on both knees." The same idea applies to the grapes that become the wine that finds its way into the chalice.

> So what the priest is doing at the altar is to separate, to earmark, this particular lump of wheat, this particular dose of grape-juice, for a supernatural destiny. And that, of course, is just what is happening to you and me all the time. Sooner or later we shall die, and that moment of death will be, please God, our Consecration; we shall be changed into something different, be given a spiritual body in place of our natural body, and live praising God among the Saints to all eternity. What we are doing now, all the time, is to make of our lives an Offertory to Almighty God; to separate them, set them apart for him, so that when death comes it may be our Consecration.

Thus "we mustn't despise…the unconsecrated host which the priest is holding up in front of the crucifix, the drops of wine which are trickling down into the chalice…. The action of the Mass is all continuous, you see, and the action of the Mass has begun."[5]

In 1957 Father Pius Parsch put it this way: "What does the priest offer? 'This spotless victim.' He offers the bread, but the expression *hostia immaculata* shows that the thoughts of the priest in this prayer do not rest here. This bread which he holds in his hands is as yet neither *hostia* (victim) nor, properly speaking, *immaculata*. Yet already he has its destiny in mind. It is to become the Eucharist, the *Hostia immaculata* in very truth, a consummation already anticipated in thought."[6]

Next comes the incensing of the bread and wine, the crucifix and the altar.

> Through the intercession of Blessed Michael the Archangel, standing at the right hand of the altar of

Sacred Then and Sacred Now

> incense, and of all His elect may the Lord vouchsafe to bless + this incense and to receive it in the odor of sweetness. Through Christ our Lord. Amen.
>
> May this incense blessed by You, arise before You, O Lord, and may Your mercy come down upon us.
>
> Let my prayer, O Lord, come like incense before You; the lifting up of my hands, like the evening sacrifice. O Lord, set a watch before my mouth, a guard at the door of my lips. Let not my heart incline to the evil of engaging in deeds of wickedness.

Now the priest himself is incensed, followed by other clergy and the servers.

> May the Lord enkindle in us the fire of His love and the flame of everlasting charity. Amen.

The people then stand to be incensed. They make a profound bow both before and after being incensed.

The priest, meanwhile, washes his hands as a sign of the purity he desires for himself as he offers the holy sacrifice. This is the Lavabo, which gets its name from the first Latin word of Psalm 25, a portion of which the priest now recites:

> I will wash my hands among the innocent, and I will encompass Thine Altar, O Lord. That I may hear the voice of praise, and tell of all Thy wondrous works. I have loved, O Lord, the beauty of Thy house, and the place where Thy glory dwelleth. Take not away my soul, O God, with the wicked, nor my life with men of blood. In whose hands are iniquities, their right hand is filled with gifts.
>
> But as for me, I have walked in my innocence; redeem me, and have mercy on me. My foot hath stood in the right way; in the churches I will bless Thee, O Lord.

After praying the Glory Be, the priest now prays the Suscipe, Sancta Trinitas:

> Receive, O Holy Trinity, this oblation which we make to Thee in memory of the Passion, Resurrection and Ascension of our Lord Jesus Christ; and in honor of

A Brief Guide to the Extraordinary Form

> Blessed Mary ever Virgin, of blessed John the Baptist, the holy Apostles Peter and Paul, of these and of all the Saints. To them let it bring honor, and to us salvation, and may they whom we are commemorating here on earth deign to plead for us in heaven. Through the same Christ our Lord. Amen.

He kisses the altar, and turning to the faithful begins to pray the Orate Fratres, the first two words of which are said in a loud voice, and completes the prayer as he turns back to the altar. This prayer will be familiar to Catholics familiar with the ordinary form of the Mass:

> Pray, brethren, that my sacrifice and yours may be acceptable to God the Father Almighty.

After the response to the Orate Fratres is made, the priest prays the Secret prayer, which is another proper that changes with each Mass. The Secret prayer is so called because it was originally the only prayer that the priest said in a low voice, and the designation has remained to the present day.[7] At the conclusion, the priest says "per omnia saecula saeculorum" audibly. The people stand.

A brief exchange with the servers and people is followed by the Preface. The Preface changes during certain parts of the liturgical year and on certain feasts; the missal has a section containing all the prefaces other than the one used on most Sundays. That one follows:

> It is truly meet and just, right for our salvation, that we should at all times and in all places, give thanks unto Thee, O holy Lord, Father almighty, everlasting God; Who, together with Thine only-begotten Son, and the Holy Ghost, art one God, one Lord: not in the oneness of a single Person, but in the Trinity of one substance. For what we believe by Thy revelation of Thy glory, the same do we believe of Thy Son, the same of the Holy Ghost, without difference or separation. So that in confessing the true and everlasting Godhead, distinction in persons,

Sacred Then and Sacred Now

> unity in essence, and equality in majesty may be adored. Which the Angels and Archangels, the Cherubim also and the Seraphim do praise, who cease not daily to cry out, with one voice, saying....

The Preface leads into the Sanctus–so named for its first three words: *Sanctus, Sanctus, Sanctus* (Holy, Holy, Holy). This is an extremely ancient prayer; St. Clement of Rome, the third Successor of St. Peter, indicates that it was being sung in church in the first century.[8] The bell is rung as the Sanctus begins. In the extraordinary form, the people kneel as the Sanctus begins, not as it ends.

We now enter the Canon of the Mass, known in the ordinary form as Eucharistic Prayer One. This so-called Roman Canon is ancient and venerable, dating in its essentials to the fifth century.

> Most merciful Father, we humbly pray and beseech Thee, through Jesus Christ Thy Son, Our Lord, to accept and to bless these + gifts, these + presents, these + holy unspotted Sacrifices, which we offer up to Thee, in the first place, for Thy Holy Catholic Church, that it may please Thee to grant her peace, to preserve, unite, and govern her throughout the world; as also for Thy servant N...our Pope, and N...our Bishop, and for all orthodox believers and all who profess the Catholic and Apostolic faith.
>
> Be mindful, O Lord, of Thy servants and handmaids N...and N...and of all here present, whose faith and devotion are known to Thee, for whom we offer, or who offer up to Thee this Sacrifice of praise for themselves and all those dear to them, for the redemption of their souls and the hope of their safety and salvation: who now pay their vows to Thee, the everlasting, living and true God.
>
> In communion with, and honoring the memory in the first place of the glorious ever Virgin Mary Mother of our God and Lord Jesus Christ; also of blessed Joseph, her Spouse; and likewise of Thy blessed Apostles and Martyrs, Peter and Paul, Andrew, James, John, Thomas,

A Brief Guide to the Extraordinary Form

> James, Philip, Bartholomew, Matthew, Simon and Thaddeus, Linus, Cletus, Clement, Sixtus, Cornelius, Cyprian, Lawrence, Chrysogonus, John and Paul, Cosmas and Damian, and of all Thy Saints. Grant for the sake of their merits and prayers that in all things we may be guarded and helped by Thy protection. Through the same Christ our Lord. Amen.

The bell is rung as the priest now extends his hands over the offering:

> O Lord, we beseech Thee, graciously to accept this oblation of our service and that of Thy whole household. Order our days in Thy peace, and command that we be rescued from eternal damnation and numbered in the flock of Thine elect. Through Christ our Lord. Amen.
>
> Humbly we pray Thee, O God, be pleased to make this same offering wholly blessed +, to consecrate + it and approve + it, making it reasonable and acceptable, so that it may become for us the Body + and Blood + of Thy dearly beloved Son, our Lord Jesus Christ.
>
> Who, the day before He suffered, took bread into His Holy and venerable hands, and having lifted up His eyes to heaven, to Thee, God, His Almighty Father, giving thanks to Thee, blessed it +, broke it, and gave it to His disciples, saying: Take and eat ye all of this.
>
> FOR THIS IS MY BODY.

Note that the priest bows as he arrives at the words of consecration, genuflects immediately thereafter upon speaking the words of consecration, and only then elevates the Host. Following the elevation he genuflects a second time. The same pattern occurs with the Chalice: the priest adores first, then elevates the Chalice, and then genuflects again.

> In like manner, after He had supped, taking also into His holy and venerable hands this goodly chalice, again giving thanks to Thee, He blessed it +, and gave it to His disciples, saying: Take and drink ye all of this.
>
> FOR THIS IS THE CHALICE OF MY BLOOD, OF THE

Sacred Then and Sacred Now

NEW AND ETERNAL TESTAMENT: THE MYSTERY OF FAITH: WHICH SHALL BE SHED FOR YOU AND FOR MANY UNTO THE REMISSION OF SINS.

From the moment of the consecration to the final ablutions (that is, the purification of the vessels used in Holy Communion), the priest does not separate his thumb and forefinger, to prevent even the smallest fragment of the Body of Christ from being profaned. Notice the slightly awkward way he holds the ciborium—he is keeping thumb and forefinger together during the distribution of Holy Communion.

He continues:

> And now, O Lord, we, Thy servants, and with us all Thy holy people, calling to mind the blessed Passion of this same Christ, Thy Son, our Lord, likewise His Resurrection from the grave, and also His glorious Ascension into heaven, do offer unto Thy most sovereign Majesty out of the gifts Thou hast bestowed upon us, a Victim + which is pure, a Victim + which is holy, a Victim + which is spotless, the holy Bread + of life eternal, and the Chalice + of everlasting Salvation.
>
> Deign to look upon them with a favorable and gracious countenance, and to accept them as Thou didst accept the offerings of Thy just servant Abel, and the sacrifice of our Patriarch Abraham, and that which Thy high priest Melchisedech offered up to Thee, a holy Sacrifice, an immaculate Victim.
>
> Humbly we beseech Thee, almighty God, to command that these our offerings be carried by the hands of Thy holy Angel to Thine Altar on high, in the sight of Thy divine Majesty, so that those of us who shall receive the most sacred Body + and Blood + of Thy Son by partaking thereof from this Altar may be filled with every grace and heavenly blessing: Through the same Christ our Lord. Amen.
>
> Be mindful, also, O Lord, of Thy servants and handmaids N...and N...who are gone before us with the sign of faith

A Brief Guide to the Extraordinary Form

and who sleep the sleep of peace. To these, O Lord, and to all who rest in Christ, grant, we beseech Thee, a place of refreshment, light and peace. Through the same Christ our Lord. Amen.

The priest now speaks aloud the words "Nobis quoque peccatoribus"—often rendered in Latin-English missals as, "To us also, [Thy] sinful servants." These words allow the faithful to find their place in the missal. Silence, such an integral part of traditional Catholic piety, makes it possible for the faithful to meditate on the mysteries of the altar, or to linger in their missals on some particularly evocative phrase or passage. The audible "nobis quoque peccatoribus" now draws them back, preparing them for the next part of the Mass.

> To us also Thy sinful servants, who put our trust in the multitude of Thy mercies, vouchsafe to grant some part and fellowship with Thy holy Apostles and Martyrs: with John, Stephen, Matthias, Barnabas, Ignatius, Alexander, Marcellinus, Peter, Felicity, Perpetua, Agatha, Lucy, Agnes, Cecilia, Anastasia, and all Thy Saints. Into their company we beseech Thee admit us, not considering our merits, but freely pardoning our offenses. Through Christ our Lord.

> By whom, O Lord, Thou dost always create, sanctify +, quicken +, bless +, and bestow upon us all these good things.

> Through Him +, and with Him +, and in Him +, is unto Thee, God the Father + Almighty, in the unity of the Holy + Ghost, all honor and glory.

> P. World without end.

> S. Amen.

The congregation now stands for the Our Father. At its conclusion, the priest prays:

> Deliver us, we beseech Thee, O Lord, from all evils, past, present and to come, and by the intercession of the Blessed and glorious ever Virgin Mary, Mother of God, together with Thy blessed apostles Peter and Paul, and

Sacred Then and Sacred Now

> Andrew, and all the Saints, + mercifully grant peace in our days, that through the bounteous help of Thy mercy we may be always free from sin, and safe from all disquiet.
>
> Through the same Jesus Christ, Thy Son our Lord, Who is God living and reigning with Thee in the unity of the Holy Ghost,
>
> P. World without end.
>
> S. Amen.
>
> P. May the peace + of the Lord be + always + with you.
>
> S. And with thy spirit.
>
> P. O Lord, Jesus Christ, Who didst say to Thine Apostles: Peace I leave you, My peace I give to you: look not upon my sins, but upon the faith of Thy Church; and deign to give her that peace and unity which is agreeable to Thy will: God Who livest and reignest world without end. Amen.

The Kiss of Peace, seen only in a Solemn High Mass, is a ritualized embrace involving the priest, deacon, and subdeacon rather than the informal series of greetings among the congregation that is an optional if widespread feature of the ordinary form of the Mass. (The Sign of Peace as it exists in the ordinary form is not really the restoration of an ancient tradition, since the Sign of Peace spoken of in early descriptions of the Christian liturgy was undertaken in a context in which the unbaptized, the heretical or schismatic, and those guilty of mortal sin, were either prohibited entry during the celebration of the sacred mysteries or relegated to a back portion of the Church. None of those people could participate in the Sign of Peace.)[9]

At the beginning (rather than at the end, as in the ordinary form) of the Agnus Dei ("Lamb of God") the people kneel. The priest then prays:

> O Lord Jesus Christ, Son of the living God, Who, by the will of the Father and the co-operation of the Holy Ghost,

A Brief Guide to the Extraordinary Form

hast by Thy death given life to the world: deliver me by this, Thy most sacred Body and Blood, from all my iniquities and from every evil; make me cling always to Thy commandments, and permit me never to be separated from Thee. Who with the same God, the Father and the Holy Ghost, livest and reignest God, world without end. Amen.

Let not the partaking of Thy Body, O Lord Jesus Christ, which I, though unworthy, presume to receive, turn to my judgment and condemnation; but through Thy mercy may it be unto me a safeguard and a healing remedy both of soul and body. Who livest and reignest with God the Father, in the unity of the Holy Ghost, God, world without end. Amen.

Taking the Host and genuflecting, the priest prays:

I will take the Bread of Heaven, and will call upon the name of the Lord.

Three times he prays the words of the centurion:

Lord, I am not worthy that Thou shouldst enter under my roof; but only say the word, and my soul shall be healed.

Just prior to consuming the Host, he prays:

May the Body of Our Lord Jesus Christ preserve my soul unto life everlasting. Amen.

Upon consuming the Host, he prays:

What return shall I make to the Lord for all the things that He hath given unto me? I will take the chalice of salvation, and call upon the Name of the Lord. I will call upon the Lord and give praise: and I shall be saved from mine enemies.

Then, before consuming the Precious Blood:

May the Blood of Our Lord Jesus Christ preserve my soul unto life everlasting. Amen.

An earlier tradition, still observed in many places, has the servers making a second confession of sins (the "second Confiteor") at this point, with the priest giving absolution just

Sacred Then and Sacred Now

prior to the people's Communion. The second Confiteor does not appear in the 1962 Missal, the most recent text of the extraordinary form, but it often persists because of its long usage.

The priest now says:

Behold the Lamb of God, behold Him Who taketh away the sins of the world.

The people say three times:

Lord, I am not worthy that Thou shouldst enter under my roof; but only say the word, and my soul shall be healed.

In the traditional Latin rite, Holy Communion is distributed on the tongue to kneeling communicants. Eucharistic ministers are not used. A server holds a paten, a plate made of precious metal, under the chins of all communicants in order to prevent profanation should the Host accidentally fall. To every communicant the priest says, "May the Body of Our Lord Jesus Christ preserve your soul unto everlasting life. Amen." The communicant does not reply, "Amen."

As in the ordinary form, at the conclusion of Holy Communion the priest purifies the vessels. But in the extraordinary form he also prays these words:

Grant, O Lord, that what we have taken with our mouth, we may receive with a pure mind; and that from a temporal gift it may become for us an everlasting remedy.

May Thy Body, O Lord, which I have received and Thy Blood which I have drunk, cleave to my inmost parts, and grant that no stain of sin remain in me; whom these pure and holy Sacraments have refreshed. Who livest and reignest world without end. Amen.

After purifying the vessels the priest proceeds to the epistle side of the altar to read the Communion antiphon, which is found in the missal among the propers for the Mass of the day. Returning to the center of the altar, the priest turns to the people:

A Brief Guide to the Extraordinary Form

P. The Lord be with you.

S. And with thy spirit.

P. Let us pray.

The priest now prays the Postcommunion prayer, which is the last of the propers. He returns to the center of the altar.

P. The Lord be with you.

S. And with thy spirit.

P. Go, the Mass is ended.

S. Thanks be to God.

The priest bows before the altar and prays the Placeat Tibi:

> May the tribute of my homage be pleasing to Thee, O most holy Trinity. Grant that the Sacrifice which I, unworthy as I am, have offered in the presence of Thy Majesty, may be acceptable to Thee. Through Thy mercy may it bring forgiveness to me and to all for whom I have offered it. Through Christ our Lord. Amen.

He turns to the people and says:

> May Almighty God bless you: the Father, + the Son, and the Holy Ghost.

The Mass now concludes with the Last Gospel, the opening verses of the Gospel of St. John, which is a philosophical reflection on the Incarnation of Christ. The recitation of the Last Gospel, which had once been a private priestly devotion after Mass, was expressly added into the missal by Pope St. Pius V in 1570. All genuflect at the words "*Et Verbum caro factum est*" ("And the Word was made flesh").

That is an all-too-brief stroll through a High Mass in the extraordinary form. At a Low Mass things will be rather different. Among other things, there will be more silence and more kneeling, fewer candles and no incense. Following the Last Gospel, moreover, a traditional Latin Low Mass con-

Sacred Then and Sacred Now

cludes with the Leonine prayers, instituted by Pope Leo XIII in the late nineteenth century: three Hail Marys, the Hail, Holy Queen, and the prayer to St. Michael the Archangel. Finally, the priest says "Most Sacred Heart of Jesus" three times, and each time the people respond, "Have mercy upon us." (This last part was added by Pope St. Pius X.)

Some people appreciate the silence of the Low Mass, since it allows them to focus intensely on their missals and to pray at Mass. I have heard this preference given voice by mothers of young children, including my own wife, who say that the peace and quiet affords them one of the few opportunities they have all week for recollected prayer. Others prefer the High Mass, with its incense, its Gregorian chant, and indeed its grandeur. Although both positions are worthy of respect, my own sympathies lie with the latter. The experience of the traditional High Mass compels the worshiper to contemplate heavenly things, and practically challenges newcomers and the curious not to be impressed and moved by it.

This is the great jewel, the pearl of great price, that Pope Benedict XVI has restored to the Catholic Church.

1. Archbishop Raymond L. Burke, "Be Not Afraid," *St. Louis Review*, July 20, 2007. Available online at http://www.stlouisreview.com/abpcolumn.php?abpid=13323 (accessed August 15, 2007).
2. Adolph Dominic Frenay, O.P., *The Spirituality of the Mass in the Light of Thomistic Theology* (St. Louis: B. Herder, 1953), 5-6.
3. Ibid., 6.
4. Michael Davies, ed., *The Wisdom of Adrian Fortescue* (Fort Collins, Colo.: Roman Catholic Books, 1999), 254.
5. See Ronald Knox, *The Mass in Slow Motion* (New York: Sheed & Ward, 1948), ch. vi.
6. Pius Parsch, *The Liturgy of the Mass* (St. Louis: B. Herder, 1957).
7. Davies, ed., *The Wisdom of Adrian Fortescue*, 318.
8. Ibid., 329.
9. Romano Tommasi, "The Construction of the New Mass," *The Latin Mass*, Summer 2002, 33-34.

Chapter 4

Important Features of the Extraordinary Form

Neither Vatican II nor the Missal of 1970 envisioned or prescribed Communion standing, Communion in the hand, Eucharistic ministers, or female altar servers, though each of these has become common in Catholic parishes over the years. None of these things occur in the extraordinary form of the Mass. None is required in the ordinary form, either, but in the extraordinary form they are absolutely excluded.

Communion on the Tongue

Celebrations according to the 1962 Missal take for granted that the communicant is to receive Holy Communion on the tongue rather than in the hand. Reception of Holy Communion on the tongue was the norm throughout the Latin Rite until 1969, when the Holy See issued an indult permitting the practice in the most difficult and disobedient Catholic countries. Later the indult was expanded. Italy did not have it until the 1980s–and Poland only two years ago.

Dietrich von Hildebrand, one of the twentieth-century's great moral theologians and Catholic writers, and deeply admired by Popes John Paul II and Benedict XVI, warned that Communion in the hand could have the effect of undermining people's faith in the Real Presence. "To be allowed to touch the consecrated host with unanointed hands is in no way presented to the faithful as an awe-inspiring privilege," he wrote in a 1973 article called "Communion in the Hand Should Be Rejected." "It becomes the normal form of receiving Communion. And this fosters an irreverent attitude and thus corrodes faith in the real bodily presence of Christ." The late theologian Father John Hardon, S.J., urged in 1997 that "whatever you can do to stop Communion in the hand will be blessed by God."[1]

In the same way that a deeper understanding of the theology of the Eucharist and the extraordinary gift God has given us helped to foster the practice of Eucharistic adoration, a fuller appreciation of Christ's Real Presence also led over time to the rejection of Communion in the hand and the adoption of Communion on the tongue. As the Congregation for Divine Worship noted in 1969, "Later, with a deepening understanding of the truth of the eucharistic mystery, of its power and of the presence of Christ in it, there came a greater feeling of reverence towards this sacrament and a deeper humility was felt to be demanded when receiving it. Thus the custom was established of the minister placing a particle of consecrated bread on the tongue of the communicant."

It was no accident that sixteenth-century Protestants like Martin Bucer insisted so strongly on the reception of Communion in the hand. Although Protestant opinion varied, the consensus held that Catholic teaching on the Real Presence amounted to gross idolatry. Encouraging Communion in the hand, they believed, undermined two Catholic teachings at once: the ministerial priesthood and the Real Presence of Christ in the Eucharist. First, the distribution of Communion in the hand implied that there was nothing special about the ordained priest, since laymen had just as much right to touch the Eucharist as he did. Second, receiving the Host in the hand emphasized that the Eucharist was ordinary bread—for if it is

Important Features of the Extraordinary Form

nothing more than ordinary bread, why shouldn't a layman be able to receive it directly in his hand?

That the practice of Communion in the hand was observed well over a millennium ago is virtually irrelevant. As Pope Pius XII explained in his 1947 encyclical *Mediator Dei*, the desire to introduce novel practices into Catholic worship when the existing practice is venerable and hallowed by tradition is at odds with a normal and healthy *sensus Catholicus*. May we apply this reproof to those Catholics in the 1960s who disobediently resurrected the discarded practice, centuries after Communion on the tongue had become the established norm?

In fact, Bishop Juan Rodolfo Laise of San Luis, Argentina, who announced in 1996 that Communion in the hand was to be forbidden in his diocese, drew this very conclusion, citing this teaching of Pius XII in support of his policy. The bishop's decision was subsequently approved by the Congregation for the Doctrine of the Faith, which informed him that "in deciding to maintain immutable the tradition of distributing Holy Communion in the mouth, [you] have acted in conformity with the law and therefore have not broken with ecclesial communion."

When Pope Paul VI grudgingly allowed Communion in the hand in 1969, his permission came in the context of a letter urging that the traditional practice of Communion on the tongue be retained. Allowance for Communion in the hand was made as a concession for parts of the world where disobedience on this point had already reached epidemic proportions. The Pontiff thus allowed the bishops to permit the practice if they thought it the best way to cope with the situation.

We read in *Memoriale Domini*, the Congregation for Divine Worship's 1969 Instruction on the Manner of Distributing Holy Communion, that a "change in a matter of such moment, based on a most ancient and venerable tradi-

Sacred Then and Sacred Now

tion, does not merely affect discipline. It carries certain dangers with it which may arise from the new manner of administering Holy Communion: the danger of a loss of reverence for the august sacrament of the altar, of profanation, of adulterating the true doctrine." For these and other reasons, the Congregation explained, "the Holy Father has decided not to change the existing way of administering Holy Communion to the faithful." The Congregation's warnings continued:

> This method of distributing Holy Communion [on the tongue] must be retained, taking the present situation of the Church in the entire world into account, not merely because it has many centuries of tradition behind it, but especially because it expresses the faithful's reverence for the Eucharist.
>
> Further, the practice which must be considered traditional ensures, more effectively, that Holy Communion is distributed with the proper respect, decorum and dignity. It removes the danger of profanation of the sacred species, in which "in a unique way, Christ, God and man, is present whole and entire, substantially and continually." Lastly, it ensures that diligent carefulness about the fragments of consecrated bread which the Church has always recommended.
>
> The Apostolic See therefore emphatically urges bishops, priests and laity to obey carefully the law which is still valid and which has again been confirmed. It urges them to take account of the judgment given by the majority of Catholic bishops, of the rite now in use in the liturgy, of the common good of the Church.

These were the urgings and warnings that preceded the Holy See's reluctant allowance for Communion in the hand in those countries where this forbidden practice had become widespread.

As we saw in chapter three, the 1962 Missal contains an edifying and very beautiful instruction to the priest: from the

Important Features of the Extraordinary Form

moment of the consecration until the final ablutions, he is to hold thumb and forefinger together, in order to prevent the profanation of any particle of the Sacred Species. If for centuries the Church taught her priests to show such fastidious devotion to Christ, then Father Hardon's desire to discourage Communion in the hand becomes a matter of simple common sense–for if priests were once concerned about Eucharistic fragments just between their thumbs and forefingers, so much greater is the problem presented by the layman who takes the entire Host into his outstretched hand.

Kneeling for Holy Communion

In the extraordinary form the faithful kneel for Holy Communion, normally at an altar rail. The abandonment of this pious practice is of very recent origin–four decades ago it was still the common manner of receiving Holy Communion.

Why shouldn't we receive Christ on our knees–as was (and in some places still is) even the traditional Lutheran posture when receiving Communion? A parish bulletin insert from several years ago employed a common argument to justify the change: "We should remember that standing itself is a gesture of reverence. It is our cultural custom to stand when a dignitary enters a room or when we sing the national anthem."[2]

To be sure, at some times and in certain places, standing was the posture that indicated the highest form of reverence. But that is not the case in modern Western culture, and so appeals to the practice of the early Church are irrelevant to the situation in the West here and now. It is surely unwise to disrupt traditional Catholic piety for the sake of introducing a gesture that is less suggestive of the kind of reverence that is owed to God alone, and more suggestive of the reverence we show when a mere "dignitary enters a room." Jesus Christ is rather more important than the ambassador from Liechtenstein.

Sacred Then and Sacred Now

In practice, having people receive the Eucharist in an ordinary way–we stand all the time, after all–rather than an unusual one (how often do we kneel, except before Christ?) can make them think that what they are receiving in Holy Communion is relatively unremarkable. This principle has often been summed up by the Latin phrase *lex orandi lex credendi*, which is normally translated as "The law of prayer is the law of belief." How we pray influences what we believe. If the words and postures by which we pray leave some question about the nature of the Mass, the offering of sacrifice, and the Real Presence of Christ, then our belief in these things is likely to grow less certain and more confused.

Cardinal Ratzinger's remarks about the value of kneeling in the liturgy are worth recalling here. Kneeling, he said, "may well be...alien to modern culture," which has "turned away from the faith, and no longer knows the One before whom kneeling is the right, indeed intrinsically necessary gesture. The man who learns to believe learns also to kneel, and a faith or a liturgy no longer familiar with kneeling would be sick at the core."[3] He also pointed out the numerous biblical examples that emphasize kneeling as the proper posture for adoration and prayer.[4] How appropriate, then, to kneel at the moment of Holy Communion.

Male Altar Servers

In the newsletter of its Committee on the Liturgy, the United States Conference of Catholic Bishops observed in mid-2007 that in the extraordinary form "only clerics or 'altar boys' perform liturgical ministry."[5] Pope John Paul II gave voice to the ancient tradition of male altar service in *Inaestimabile Donum* (1980), where he declared that "women are not...permitted to act as altar servers."[6] The Pope cited *Liturgicae Instaurationes* (1970), an Instruction of the Congregation for Divine Worship, which declared, "In conform-

Important Features of the Extraordinary Form

ity with norms traditional in the Church, women (single, married, religious)...are barred from serving the priest at the altar."[7]

In 1994 female altar servers were suddenly permitted for use in the ordinary form of the Roman rite. But this concession, according to Msgr. John F. McCarthy, founder of the Oblates of Wisdom, came in the form of an indult–that is, an exception to a general rule–and one that bishops were at liberty to forbid in their dioceses. "The implication is that the general liturgical norm prohibiting female altar servers remains in existence, so that in general women may not serve at the altar *unless* a local ordinary intervenes by a positive act and grants permission for his territorial jurisdiction. Thus, the Congregation [for Divine Worship] has clarified the authentic interpretation to mean that an *indult* is given to diocesan bishops to permit the use of female servers."[8] Instruction number 2 of the indult itself urges that "it will always be very appropriate to follow the noble tradition of having boys serve at the altar."

Perhaps the best analysis of and argument against female altar servers comes from Fr. Brian Harrison, a professor of theology at the Pontifical University of Puerto Rico.[9] The very fact that the exclusively male preserve of altar service can be traced back to the beginning of the Church weighs very heavily in the equation, particularly for a Church that values Tradition as one of its pillars. Writes Fr. Harrison: "In the case of a religious tradition which has not only existed, but has been consciously, continuously, and emphatically reaffirmed and insisted upon for two millennia, there must be an enormous and overwhelming presumption that such a tradition reflects the will of Christ." According to liturgical scholar Aimé-Georges Martimort, writing in the Vatican journal *Notitiae*, the "general discipline of the Church [against female altar service] has been set in stone by canon 44 of the

Sacred Then and Sacred Now

Collection of Laodicea which dates generally from the end of the 4th century and which has figured in almost all canonical collections of East and West."

Many of the arguments against female altar servers are similar to those that justify the reservation of the priesthood to men alone, particularly since altar servers are often considered extensions of the priest. (Arguments in defense of a male-only priesthood are well summarized in Pope John Paul II's Apostolic Letter *Ordinatio Sacerdotalis* and the Congregation for the Doctrine of the Faith's 1976 document *Inter Insigniores*, both of which are available online.) We see this close relationship between altar service and its culmination in the priesthood not only in that both the priest and alter servers wear the cassock and surplice, but also in certain linguistic conventions. The Spanish word for altar boy is *monaguillo*, which means a "little monk." In Italian, adds Father Harrison, "the word for altar boy is *chierichetto*—a 'little cleric,' which means that the term used naturally for 'altar girls' in Italian is in itself an affront to Catholic doctrine: they are called *donne chierichetto*, 'little *female* clerics.'"

A married person, according to Catholic teaching as well as common sense, may not flirt or become involved romantically with a member of the opposite sex even if their relationship should remain technically chaste. Their behavior toward each other is logically ordered toward physical consummation even if such consummation does not in fact occur.

Father Harrison draws an analogy between this example and female altar service, since both involve an unbecoming flirtation with an outcome that divine law forbids. "From this perspective," he writes, "we could say that a woman or girl serving at the altar, no matter how devout her personal intentions, no matter how reverent, recollected and modest her deportment and dress, is by her very presence in the sanctu-

Important Features of the Extraordinary Form

ary engaging in what is objectively a kind of spiritual immodesty. She is flirting, as it were, with priestly ordination—mimicking it, drawing as near as she can to it with an indecorous familiarity and an intrusive intimacy. Her liturgical role insinuates and suggests ordination as its proper goal or fulfillment, even though this is absolutely excluded by the Law of Christ."

Female altar service, in short, introduces "a deep tension, an inner contradiction, into the sacred liturgy. It makes an ideological statement which both politicizes and secularizes our Eucharistic worship. Instead of reflecting the sublime harmony of the communion of saints, a foretaste of Heaven itself, the sanctuary comes to symbolize an earthly battlefield in the new cold war against 'patriarchy.'"

Eucharistic Ministers Not Used

In the extraordinary form, the distribution of Holy Communion is confined to the ordained priest (or, in rare cases, to deacons who are on their way to becoming priests). Lay ministers of the Eucharist are not used.

This aspect will no doubt seem jarring to those who have grown accustomed to the sight of laymen flocking into the sanctuary in order to function as "Eucharistic ministers." But for one thing, this practice was supposed to be rare even in the ordinary form of the Mass—hence the official title "*extraordinary* [in the sense of unusual] ministers of the Eucharist." More importantly, the beautiful practice of receiving Holy Communion at the hands of a priest plays an important role in reinforcing priestly identity and gives meaning to the discipline of celibacy observed throughout the Roman Rite.

Father James McLucas, former Christendom College chaplain and a priest of the Archdiocese of New York, wrote an extended and important reflection on this subject in 1998. The celibate Catholic priest, who gives up the holy estate of mar-

Sacred Then and Sacred Now

riage and an exclusive relationship with an earthly spouse in order to devote himself to God's service, was traditionally consoled by an exclusive relationship of his own: he alone could touch God. "The traditional role of the celibate priest as the sole administrator of the sacred," Fr. McLucas explained, "assisted him in sublimating his natural desire for exclusivity with another in marriage, and preserved his orientation toward his spiritual espousal to the Church and his spiritual fatherhood."[10]

The priest does not lose his normal human need for an exclusive relationship with another simply because he is a priest. But while other people satisfy this need through marriage, the priest finds it in his exclusive custodianship of the Eucharist–"an incomparable and unparalleled intimacy" with God, as Fr. McLucas put it. When laymen touch the Host, they (unwittingly, no doubt) deprive him of this exclusivity, which is supposed to ground and give strength to his celibate commitment.

Furthermore, the paternal dimension of the priesthood–the priest's role as spiritual father–is undermined when the priest is in effect told that after the consecration he is really no longer needed; the laity can take things from there. "The act of the priest 'feeding' the faithful with the Bread of Life incarnates his role as Its sole provider and, far more than the eye can see, forms his and his people's perception of his spiritual fatherhood," wrote Fr. McLucas. And young boys are less likely to pursue priestly vocations, or indeed to be intrigued by and attracted to the priestly office in the first place, if the priest is not a figure of awe, who alone brings his people the divine gifts. If Mrs. Jones can do practically everything he can, young men will be less likely to be willing to make the sacrifices associated with the priesthood.

Important Features of the Extraordinary Form

1. John Hardon, S.J., Call to Holiness conference, Detroit, Michigan, November 1, 1997.
2. Dennis C. Smolarski, S.J., "What Is the Gesture of Reverence for Communion, and How Does It Take Place?" Catechetical Bulletin Insert on the 2002 General Instruction of the Roman Missal and the Order of Mass, Minneapolis-St. Paul Archdiocese, 2002.
3. Cardinal Joseph Ratzinger, *The Spirit of the Liturgy*, trans. John Saward (San Francisco: Ignatius Press, 2000), 194.
4. Ibid., 188-93.
5. "Nine Questions on the Ordinary and Extraordinary Forms of the *Missale Romanum*," *United States Conference of Catholic Bishops Committee on the Liturgy Newsletter*, May/June 2007, 27.
6. John Paul II, *Inaestimabile Donum* 18.
7. Congregation for Divine Worship, *Liturgicae Instaurationes* 7.
8. John F. McCarthy, "The Canonical Meaning of the Recent Authentic Interpretation of Canon 230.2 Regarding Female Altar Servers," *Fellowship of Catholic Scholars Newsletter*, December 1994, 15.
9. The quotations that follow come from Brian W. Harrison, O.S., "'Altar Girls': Feminist Ideology and the Roman Liturgy," *Living Tradition*, July 2000, http://www.rtforum.org/lt/lt88.html.
10. This section is deeply indebted to an extraordinary article: Fr. James McLucas, "The Emasculation of the Priesthood," *The Latin Mass*, Spring 1998, available at http://www.latinmassmagazine.com/articles/articles_emasculation.html

Chapter 5

Common Misconceptions

The same handful of objections always arises when someone mentions the extraordinary form of the Roman rite. This chapter replies to those objections.

"Having Mass in Latin doesn't make sense—nobody speaks Latin."

One could cite a great many popes on the use of the Latin language, but consider just these two, each of whom reigned within living memory. First, Pius XI: "For the Church, precisely because it embraces all nations and is destined to endure to the end of time...of its very nature requires a language which is universal, immutable, and non-vernacular."[1] Pope John XXIII quoted this passage in his own Apostolic Letter on Latin, *Veterum Sapientia* (1962). He himself wrote: "Finally, the Catholic Church has a dignity far surpassing that of every merely human society, for it was founded by Christ the Lord. It is altogether fitting, therefore, that the language it uses should be noble, majestic, and non-vernacular."

Consider what a sublime teaching that is. The Catholic Church has a dignity far surpassing that of every merely human society, and therefore, as befits this dignity, it should employ a language that is the unique possession of no single group of people. The Church has never condemned harmless

Sacred Then and Sacred Now

regional variations, which are bound to exist: devotional practices more popular in one place than another, particular saints enjoying greater devotion in some places than in others, and so on. But when we step into our churches, it is good for us to leave outside much of what differentiates us as Americans, Canadians, Frenchmen, or Koreans, so that we might better appreciate what we share in common as Catholics. What a shame it is to turn our backs on this beautiful expression of the universality of the Church in order that we might enjoy the familiarity of our own language.

By preserving Latin as the liturgical language of the Roman Rite, therefore, not only do we erect a barrier against improvisation and heresy (in the form of questionable translations) but we also give expression to our identity as Catholics. We may not speak any Latin ourselves—though it is highly desirable that Catholics learn this sacred language—and rely entirely on our missals to navigate the Mass. But a liturgical language common to us all reminds us that we belong to an institution greater than any nation, and one that binds us to the faithful all over the world. The whole world is our mission territory, and it is entirely fitting that we missionaries, bound together as members of the Mystical Body of Christ, should worship in a common language.

Observe how Pope Pius XII described Gregorian chant, which is so evocative of the universality of the Church, in 1955:

> It is the duty of all those to whom Christ the Lord has entrusted the task of guarding and dispensing the Church's riches to preserve this precious treasure of Gregorian chant diligently and to impart it generously to the Christian people.... And if in Catholic churches throughout the entire world Gregorian chant sounds forth without corruption or diminution, the chant itself, like the sacred Roman liturgy, will have a characteristic of universality, so that the faithful, wherever they may be,

Common Misconceptions

will hear music that is familiar to them and a part of their own home. In this way they may experience, with much spiritual consolation, the wonderful unity of the Church. This is one of the most important reasons why the Church so greatly desires that the Gregorian chant traditionally associated with the Latin words of the sacred liturgy be used.[2]

Vatican II urged that "the use of the Latin language is to be preserved in the Latin rites."[3] The Council likewise emphasized how important it was for the faithful to "be able to say or to sing together in Latin those parts of the Ordinary of the Mass which pertain to them."[4]

The use of a non-vernacular tongue is not an uncommon religious phenomenon. Islam uses Arabic even in non-Arabic-speaking parts of the world, and synagogue services are largely in Hebrew–a tongue that has only recently begun once again to be used as a vernacular language. Although Christ read the Scriptures in Hebrew, the language of the Palestinian Jews in his day was Aramaic. (In the name of fostering "active participation," Reform Judaism once tried, unsuccessfully, to displace Hebrew, which has since returned to the Reform liturgy.)

The unity that Latin symbolizes and fosters has proven irresistibly attractive to a great many converts. Consider the example of Douglas Hyde (1911-1981), who worked for the Communist Party for two decades and edited its British newspaper, the *Daily Worker*. Hyde had sought in secular ideologies a cure for the divisions that afflicted the postwar world. "The generation which came to manhood between the wars–my generation–pagan though it was, grew up in the belief that some sort of universal harmony and lasting peace was possible, that men need not remain divided." Hyde and his colleagues had looked in vain to secular organizations to supply this unity. "We looked to the new organizations to achieve this for us–some to the League of Nations, some to world

Sacred Then and Sacred Now

Communism," he wrote. None lived up to expectations: "The League of Nations has been dead, murdered, for eight years. No one has the same hopes of the United Nations or, if they ever had, bitter reality has long since brought disillusionment. The Communist International, far from uniting the human race, is splitting it both horizontally [into East versus West] and vertically [into property owners versus proletariat]...."

For a variety of reasons, including his interest in the medieval world, Hyde began to inquire into Catholicism. Then something impressed itself upon him:

> At 11:30 p.m. on Christmas Eve I was twiddling the knob of my radio. Unable to get out to Midnight Mass I wanted at least to bring it to my fireside. And as I switched from one European station to the next I tuned in to one Midnight Mass after the other. Belgium, France, Germany, Eire, yes, even behind the Iron Curtain, Prague. It seemed as though the whole of what was once Christendom was celebrating what is potentially the most unifying event in man's history. And the important thing was that it was the same Mass. I am a newcomer to the Mass but I was able to recognize its continuity as I went from station to station for it was in one common language. This aspect of Catholicism is but a single one, and maybe not the most important. But I have a strong feeling that it is precisely the Catholicism of the Catholic Church which may prove the greatest attraction, and will meet the greatest need, for my disillusioned generation.[5]

Hyde, who converted to Catholicism in 1948, traveled extensively throughout Asia during the 1950s. In his ensuing book *One Front Across the World* (1956) he wrote about those travels, where time and again he witnessed the simplest of folk actively praying the traditional Latin Mass. He told a story from Korea in which a Msgr. Thomas Quinlan had wanted to start a choir for his cathedral. The monsignor recruited a pagan professor of music and seventy of his stu-

Common Misconceptions

dents, none of whom were Catholic (this was genuine mission territory) and taught them how to pronounce ecclesiastical Latin. Soon they were practicing the music for High Mass.

When the time came for Bishop Patrick J. Byrne to be consecrated in Seoul, Hyde relates, the professor went to the consecration "and was enormously impressed by the Church's liturgy. It was, he said, the nearest thing to heaven he had ever experienced, and the Cistercian *Salve Regina* was the most perfect piece of music he had ever heard. He came into the Church a convert and before long the students in the choir, one after another, came in too."

And they didn't speak Latin–or any language derived from it.

In 1923 even the acerbic H.L. Mencken, no Catholic he, conceded a certain respect for the Catholic Church and the Mass: "The Latin Church, which I constantly find myself admiring, despite its frequent astounding imbecilities, has always kept clearly before it the fact that religion is not a syllogism, but a poem.... Rome, indeed, has not only preserved the original poetry of Christianity; it has also made capital additions to that poetry–for example, [to] the poetry...of the liturgy itself." "A solemn High Mass," he concluded, "must be a thousand times as impressive, to a man with any genuine religious sense in him, as the most powerful sermon ever roared under the big-top." Mencken warned that a day might come "when some extra-bombastic deacon will astound humanity and insult God by proposing to translate the liturgy into American, that all the faithful may be convinced by it."

As rumors of the Pope's *motu proprio* liberating the 1962 Missal began to surface, Jewish columnist Barbara Kay, who attends an all-Hebrew service at her synagogue, explained her own partiality toward the use of Latin in the Mass: "The power of liturgy to lift us out of our narrow practical and material pursuits is not dependent on our understanding of every actual word we are saying, any more than our emotional submission to classical music's soaring magic is dependent on our ability to read the score that produced it.... An ancestral, globally employed language like Hebrew or Latin provides a context for predictable and organic communion amongst those present at the service. Through regular engagement, even though rote, with a universally recognized language, worshippers are subliminally imbued with a common motivational narrative from the past, common moral goals in the present and intimations of a common destiny in the future."[6]

Barbara Kay concluded her article for Canada's *National Post* with a simple wish: "Bring back the Latin Mass."[7]

Father Adrian Fortescue, one of the twentieth century's greatest liturgical experts, contributed the vast bulk of the liturgical articles that appeared in the 1913 *Catholic Encyclopedia*. And he insisted on the importance of Latin. "The use of Latin all over the Roman patriarchate is a very obvious and splendid witness of unity. Every Catholic traveler in a country of which he does not know the language has felt the comfort of finding that in church at least everything is familiar and knows that in a Catholic church of his own rite he is at home anywhere." Any "change of liturgical language would be a break with the past. It is a witness of antiquity of which a Catholic may well be proud that in Mass today we are still used to the very words that Anselm, Gregory, Leo sang in their cathedrals." The results for music, he said, would likewise be disastrous, for it would "abolish Latin chant." "Plainsong, as venerable a relic of antiquity as any part of the ritual, is composed for the Latin text only, supposes always the Latin syllables and the Latin accent, and becomes a caricature when it is forced into another language with different rules of accent."[8]

The introduction of the vernacular, whereby Latin, a sym-

Common Misconceptions

bol of the universal Church, gives way to a massive retreat into our national groupings, can cut us off from fellow members of the Church Militant throughout the world. Cardinal Alfons Stickler, prefect emeritus of the Vatican library and archives and a *peritus* (expert) on Vatican II's Liturgy Commission, reminds us that there was once a time when a priest could have said Mass anywhere in the world. There was also a time when Catholics could have attended Mass around the world and found it the same Mass with which they were familiar—a profoundly moving testimony to their membership in a universal, supernatural organization. "By introducing the exclusive use of the vernacular," Stickler notes, "the reform makes out of the unity of the Church a variety of little churches, separated and isolated. Where is the pastoral possibility for Catholics across the whole world to find their Mass, to overcome racial differences through a common language of worship, or even, in an increasingly small world, simply to be able to pray together, as the Council explicitly calls for? Where is the pastoral practicability now for every priest to exercise the highest priestly act—Holy Mass—everywhere, above all in a world that is short of priests?"[9]

The complete vernacularization of the Mass would certainly not have been approved by the Council fathers. Cardinal Stickler recalls an incident at the Council in which a Sicilian bishop rose "and implored the fathers to allow caution and reason to reign on this point, because otherwise there would be the danger that the entire Mass might be held in the language of the people—whereupon the entire hall burst into uproarious laughter."[10]

"No one understood the Mass in the old days."

This strange claim flies in the face of the countless testimonies of those Catholics still with us today who recall the pre-conciliar Church from personal experience. In addition,

Sacred Then and Sacred Now

anyone suggesting such a thing expects us to believe the following: 1) literate men and women could not follow a simple Latin-English missal; 2) for years on end, no one possessed even the modest level of ambition it would have taken to ask a priest, or even an informed fellow parishioner, to explain to him the meaning of the ceremony his religion required him to attend at least once a week throughout his entire life; and 3) no one could be bothered to leaf through even one of the many books, including Maria Montessori's *The Mass Explained to Children*, that explained the basic contours of the Mass in simple language. What kind of lifeless automatons would Catholics have had to be for all this to be true?

Novelist Evelyn Waugh was much closer to the truth. "In the old Mass," he wrote, "a glance at the altar was enough to inform me of the precise stage of the liturgy. The priest's voice was often inaudible and unintelligible. I do not write with the pride of a classical scholar. Indeed I know less Latin now than I did 45 years ago. But it did not require any high state of prayer to unite oneself to the action of the priest." The emphasis on external "participation" did not serve to heighten this very real union with the actions taking place at the altar. "Repeatedly standing up and saying 'And with you' detracts from this relatively intimate association and 'participation.'"[11]

New York's Cardinal Edward Egan recently shared a revealing anecdote from a June 2007 fundraising dinner he attended on behalf of Catholic schools that educate children with physical or emotional disabilities.

> One of the more than 600 guests approached the dais toward the end of the dinner and began...to recite the responses of the altar server to the opening prayers of the traditional Latin Mass. On my right was one of the most prominent labor leaders in the nation and on my left one of the most successful construction company executives in New York. Together they joined in with the man who

had approached the dais, reciting every word with remarkable accuracy. And when they were done, the man on my right launched into the longest of the altar server's prayers in the Latin liturgy, the so-called "Suscipiat." Both got even the most difficult pronunciations correct, and it was clear from the looks on their faces and the sound of their voices that what they had recited by heart had a very special place in the heart of each of them.[12]

One of the arguments both on behalf of the Missal of 1970 and in favor of the abandonment of Latin was that people would understand the Mass better and derive greater spiritual fruits from it if they heard it in their own language. Whatever superficial plausibility that argument may have had, the results are in and the news isn't good. The vast majority of Catholics aged 18 to 44 are unable to identify their Church's teaching on the Eucharist from a list of several options. By and large they lack even the slightest idea of what the Mass is. In seven years of teaching Western civilization at the college level I encountered not a single student, out of the thousands I had in class, who was able to define the Mass as the re-presentation of Christ's Sacrifice on Calvary.

The older missal was no obstacle to conversions, either–on the contrary, the pre-conciliar Church in America saw fantastic levels of conversion, such that anti-Catholic propagandists like Paul Blanshard worried in the 1950s that the United States might become a Catholic country. According to Peter Huff, in the decades preceding Vatican II the Church in America "witnessed such a steady stream of notable literary conversions that the statistics tended to support Calvert Alexander's hypothesis of something suggesting a cultural trend."[13]

Could it be that people understood the Mass after all?

"Didn't the new liturgy aim at the laity's 'active participation' in the Mass, and isn't that a worthy goal?"

In its document on the sacred liturgy, the Second Vatican

Sacred Then and Sacred Now

Council employed the Latin phrase *participatio actuosa*, which is normally translated as "active participation," to describe the ideal relationship between the laity and the liturgical rites. What exactly did the Council fathers mean by the term?

For one thing, Vatican II was not the first Church authority to speak of *participatio actuosa*; the phrase was actually introduced by Pope St. Pius X in 1903 in the *motu proprio Tra le Sollecitudini* on sacred music. "We deem it necessary to provide before anything else for the sanctity and dignity of the temple," the Pope urged, "in which the faithful assemble for no other object than that of acquiring [the true Christian] spirit from its foremost and indispensable font, which is the active participation in the most sacred mysteries and in the public and solemn prayer of the Church." For St. Pius X, active participation was a component of a larger restoration of sacred music. He wanted worshipers to sing Gregorian chant "so that they may again take a more active part in the sacred liturgy, as was the case in ancient times." (Pope Pius XI likewise urged the faithful to "participate more actively in divine worship" by singing Gregorian chant; they should not be "merely detached and silent spectators, but filled with a deep sense of the beauty of the Liturgy.")[14]

Baylor University's Professor Michael Foley reflects on St. Pius X's teaching on active participation:

> First, [active participation] is ordered towards a broader understanding or contemplation of divine things, e.g., the realities to which the chants point. This contemplation, it should be noted, takes place *through* the activity of chanting. Second, it is a participation not only in the liturgy ("the public prayer of the Church") but in the mysteries, which denotes entrance into the divine rather than mere ritual performance. Third, the fostering of active participation is to happen without changing a single word, rubric, or architectural feature. On the con-

Common Misconceptions

trary, the faithful are enjoined to rediscover and sing the existing liturgical texts.[15]

To those who insisted on more "participation" in the Mass, Evelyn Waugh answered: "'Participation' in the Mass does not mean hearing our own voice. It means God hearing our voices. Only He knows who is 'participating' at Mass. I believe, to compare small things with great, that I 'participate' in a work of art when I study it and love it silently. No need to shout."[16] The late Msgr. Richard J. Schuler, former editor of *Sacred Music*, explained it this way: "Listening is a truly active participation. Listening both to the proclaimed word and the performed music can be full, conscious and active participation. The same can be said for watching the ceremonial as it is enacted."[17] Dom Alcuin Reid, the great liturgical expert, describes active participation as "essentially contemplative."[18] Finally, as Professor Foley helpfully puts it, "The opposite of liturgical inactivity is not external activity but the internal wonder born of experiencing beauty."[19]

Some people assume that the silence that often characterizes the extraordinary form of the Roman rite precludes lay participation. But silence offers us the opportunity to focus our hearts and prayers on the action taking place at the altar, and to unite ourselves fervently to that action. Father Kenneth Myers, who was ordained in the Diocese of Pittsburgh in 1980, offered an interesting reflection in 2007 about the spiritual benefits that we reap from silence at Mass. And he is speaking not just of the Low Mass, in which the silence is very pronounced, but also of the High Mass, whose "chant and polyphony and comings and goings of the celebrant and altar boys, provides silence for the faithful so that the 'actual' participation so prized by Vatican II is available to all those who are willing to enter into interior silence and commune with the Lord."

Sacred Then and Sacred Now

> It is difficult for modern man to endure silence because we are surrounded by noise that is ever louder and louder. We fear silence because it may force us in unguarded moments to introspection and self-examination. The noise with which we have surrounded ourselves hides us from ourselves. Silence in the Mass is perhaps the greatest need of modern man because we so desperately need to peer into our souls, to enter into our own hearts, and to see there what God Himself sees. In the silence of the traditional Latin Mass we can listen to God's voice within us.
>
> The silence of the traditional Latin Mass reveals so clearly that the Mass is *not* the work of the congregation, a performance which we manufacture in order to make God happy with us. Rather, the Mass is the work of God–it is Christ's Own work of redemption carried out in our midst, on our altar. The Mass is not fabricated by man, it must be received in faith, and silence enables us to do just that: just as we do not "take" Holy Communion, but rather "receive" the Lord in the Sacrament, so do we receive Christ's redemption in the Mass.

Father Myers concluded, "May I venture to say that the traditional rite of Mass is very attuned to the needs of modern men and women because its long periods of silence are great blessings in our noisy and profane world."[20]

Cardinal Stickler, who served on Vatican II's liturgy commission, spoke of

> the various false interpretations–and equally false implementations–of a central demand of the reformers: a fervent, active participation of the faithful in the celebration of the Mass. The main purpose of their participation is what the Council expressly says: the worship of the majesty of God. The heart and soul of the participant must therefore first and foremost be raised to God. (This does not exclude the possibility that participation also becomes activated within the community.) Above all, this *actuosa participatio* was demanded as a result of the frequently lamented apathy of Mass-goers of the pre-concil-

Common Misconceptions

iar period. If it extends itself into an endless talking and doing, which allows all to become active in a kind of hustle and bustle which are intrinsic to every external human assembly, even the most holy moment of the individual's encounter with the Eucharistic God-Man becomes the most talkative and distracted. The contemplative mysticism of the encounter with God and His worship, to say nothing of the reverence which must always accompany it, instantly dies: the human element kills the divine, and fills heart and soul with emptiness and disappointment.[21]

When we properly understand the nature of the Mass, and when we consider the phrase *participatio actuosa* in the light of tradition, we realize that what we most want to encourage is that interior participation that alone inflames our spiritual lives. In the wake of *Summorum Pontificum* even a few bishops, evidently stung by the Pope's encouragement of the old liturgy, insinuated that before the introduction of the Missal of Paul VI the faithful had been mere spectators at Mass. But physical expressiveness is only one part of participation, and not the most important. What matters most is that we unite our minds and souls to the action taking place at the altar. No rite can do that for us, no matter how many outward gestures or spoken words it calls for.

Pope Benedict XVI, while Cardinal Ratzinger, spoke about this essential interior dimension of liturgical participation. The action that the worshiper performs in the liturgy, he wrote, does not consist "only or primarily in the alternation of standing, sitting and kneeling, but in inner processes. It is these which give rise to the whole drama of the liturgy. 'Let us pray–this is an invitation to share in a movement which reaches down into our inner depths. 'Lift up your hearts'–this phrase and the movement which accompanies it are, so to speak, only the 'tip of the iceberg.' The real action takes place in the deep places of men's hearts, which are lifted up to the heights."[22]

Sacred Then and Sacred Now

On another occasion, Cardinal Ratzinger invited his readers to consider exactly what the action is in which we are called to participate. According to the Fathers, he said, the *actio* of the liturgy is the Eucharistic prayer. This is the fundamental liturgical act. That may seem paradoxical: how can the laity participate in the Eucharistic prayer, whose words of consecration must be uttered by an ordained priest in order to be effectual? For one thing, we should recall that it is *God* who performs the miracle at the altar; it is Christ the High Priest who acts through his human minister, and that in an important sense no human being at all, not even a priest, actually *performs* the action. What we are to do, rather, and what amounts to the ultimate liturgical action, is to *unite ourselves* to the action of the priest, the *alter Christus*, at the altar, and to "pray for it to become *our* sacrifice." Participation in the liturgy means, above all else, our interior union with the holy sacrifice. "The uniqueness of the Eucharistic liturgy," Ratzinger wrote, "lies precisely in the fact that God himself is acting and that we are drawn into that action of God." Anything else, any external word or gesture, is absolutely secondary to this primary liturgical goal to which our minds and souls should be directed. Our failure to realize this, and our continuing emphasis on external actions rather than interior union with the Eucharistic sacrifice as the essence of participation, is a sign that "liturgical education today, of both priests and laity, is deficient to a deplorable extent."[23]

"In the extraordinary form the priest has his back to the people."

I once heard the story of a parishioner who, having seen his parish priest offer Mass according to the Missal of 1962 for the first time, approached him afterward and said, "Father, you turned your back on me!"

To which the priest replied, "It isn't about *you*, Joe."

Common Misconceptions

This incident illustrates an important point. The complaint that the priest has his "back to the people" in the extraordinary form is emblematic of a modern mentality in which "the people," rather than God, are the center of the Mass. It is also a profound misunderstanding of what is really taking place: the priest does not turn his back on the people, but instead the priest and the people *face the same direction together*.

It has long been part of Christian tradition to face east during prayer. (Masses in which priest and people face a common eastward direction are referred to as *ad orientem* Masses.) According to Cardinal Ratzinger, "Facing east means that when one prays, one is turned toward the rising sun, which has now become a subject of historical significance. It points to the Paschal Mystery of Jesus Christ, to his death and new rising. It points to the future of the world and the consummation of all history in the final coming of the redeemer."[24]

(Although the extraordinary form of Mass is necessarily said with the priest facing east, the rubrics even of the Missal of 1970 assume that the priest is facing east, with instructions at various parts of the rite directing him to turn towards the people.)

Scholars have come to acknowledge that Mass facing the people was not the primitive practice, and that Mass said *ad orientem* has in fact been the historic norm since the days of the early Church. Cardinal Ratzinger joined his voice to this scholarly consensus: "As I have written in my books, I think that celebration turned towards the east, towards the Christ who is coming, is an apostolic tradition."[25] Tertullian spoke of the practice at the end of the second century, and around the same time Clement of Alexandria offered a biblically rich reflection on the rationale for this posture. In the third century Origen likewise offered a lengthy explanation of prayer facing east.[26] Roman basilicas in which the priest might appear to

Sacred Then and Sacred Now

have traditionally "faced the people" can be accounted for simply by their peculiar construction, which forced him to face that way in order to fix his gaze eastward. (During the consecration, the people turned to face east along with the priest.)[27]

Pope Benedict has referred numerous times to the beautiful and fitting tradition whereby priest and people face the same direction. As early as 1967 Ratzinger was already asking, "Is it so absolutely important to be able to look the priest in the face, or might it not be often very salutary to reflect that he also is a Christian and that he has every reason to turn to God with all his fellow-Christians of the congregation and to say together with them 'Our Father'?"[28] By the 1990s, Cardinal Ratzinger was speaking of the desirability of returning to *ad orientem* celebrations. "Wherever possible, we should definitely take up again the apostolic tradition of facing the east, both in the building of churches and in the celebration of the liturgy."[29] He later wrote the preface to Uwe Michael Lang's book *Turning Towards the Lord: Orientation in Liturgical Prayer*, which advanced historical and theological arguments in favor of Masses *ad orientem*. "The common direction of priest and people is intrinsically fitting and proper to the liturgical action," Ratzinger explained.[30]

Why the eastward posture? For one thing, numerous biblical references in support of eastward prayer have been found.[31] Moreover, the rising sun in the east has served to symbolize the risen Christ as well as hope in His Second Coming.[32] According to Father Lang:

> There is no doubt that, from very early times, it was a matter of course for Christians all over the known world to turn in prayer towards the rising sun, that is to say, towards the geographical east. In private and in liturgical prayer Christians turned, no longer towards the earthly Jerusalem, but towards the new, heavenly Jerusalem; they believed firmly that when the Lord came again in glory to

Common Misconceptions

judge the world, he would gather his elect to make up this heavenly city. The rising sun was considered an appropriate expression of this eschatological hope.[33]

Since the Mass is a sacrifice offered to God, it stands to reason, as Fr. J.A. Jungmann observed, that the priest should in effect face God with the people as he offers it.[34] As a matter of fact, those areas of the world in which the sacrificial nature of the Mass was best developed and understood are also those in which the eastward posture of the priest was most firmly established.

Father Joseph D. Santos, Jr., a priest of the Diocese of Providence, Rhode Island, offers perhaps the most straightforward explanation of the traditional practice: "When a general leads his troops into battle does he face them? When a representative of the people approaches the Ruler on their behalf does he face them? When a priest is going to the Lord on behalf of his people should he face them? When the priest is acting as the intermediary between the people and God he faces the altar. When he is dispensing the gifts of God, or speaking to the people, he faces the people."[35]

The practice of Mass facing the people lacks this sense of a common journey forward and implies instead a closed circle, a self-contained celebration. Cardinal Ratzinger once described the practice of Mass facing the people as "an arrangement that hardly shows the liturgy to be open to the things that are above and to the world to come."[36]

"The new Mass is what Vatican II called for."

In fact, we have the testimony of numerous Council fathers to the contrary. The research of Father Brian Harrison of the Pontifical University of Puerto Rico has shown that most bishops at Vatican II envisioned only minor changes to the Mass. Monsignor Klaus Gamber, whose book *The Reform of the Roman Liturgy* features a preface by the man who

Sacred Then and Sacred Now

became Pope Benedict XVI, argued vigorously against the idea that the new Mass was a faithful implementation of the desires of the Council fathers:

> Although the argument is used over and over again by the people responsible for creating the new Mass, they cannot claim that what they have done is what the Council actually wanted. The instructions given by the Liturgy Commission were general in nature, and they opened up many possible ways for implementing what the Commission had stipulated, but one statement we can make with certainty is that the new *Ordo* of the Mass that has now emerged would not have been endorsed by the majority of the Council Fathers.[37]

According to Cardinal Darío Castrillón Hoyos, prefect of the Pontifical Commission Ecclesia Dei and former prefect of the Congregation for the Clergy, "The Council had not asked for the creation of a new rite."[38] Just before voting for the article of *Sacrosanctum Concilium* calling for a reform of the *Ordo Missae*, the Council fathers were assured by Vatican II's Liturgical Commission: "The current *Ordo Missae*, which has grown up in the course of the centuries, is to be retained." Alcuin Reid, liturgical scholar and Benedictine, asks: "What honest historian who puts the preconciliar *Ordo Missae* beside that promulgated in 1969 can say that this seemingly incredible assurance was honored?"[39]

In 1996, Reid sought the opinions of some of the remaining Council fathers on the subject of the liturgy. Speaking of the conciliar debate on the liturgy, Ignatius Doggett, emeritus Bishop of Aitape, New Guinea, insisted that "very few bishops would be proud to say they had a hand in it.... In my opinion the Debate on the Liturgy has been hijacked. The Council was...to *reform*, not to *change completely*."[40]

Another Council father, the late Cardinal Raúl Francisco Primatesta (who was Archbishop of Cordoba at the time of his

Common Misconceptions

death and Bishop of San Rafael during the Council), put it this way: "I think that the postconciliar Consilium for liturgical reform was looking to keep to the decreed conciliar line, but...*in various places* they permitted or made or introduced experiences of the *time* or went further away from the decree and spirit of the Council."[41]

Still another, Bishop Nicola Maria Agnozzi, an auxiliary of the Diocese of Ndola (Zambia) during the Council, testified that "changes were asked if necessary but nothing drastic.... There are reasons to believe that the Consilium went beyond what was contained in the decree.... I don't think the Consilium did always take into consideration the wishes of the Council in their decisions."[42]

Cardinal Stickler likewise believed that the new missal departed from the Council's intent. He had been involved so intimately in the workings of the Liturgy Commission that he could declare in his memoir, "I understood precisely...the wishes of the Council fathers, as well as the correct sense of the texts that the Council voted on and adopted."

> You can understand my astonishment when I found that the final edition of the new Roman Missal in many ways did not correspond to the conciliar texts that I knew so well, and that it contained much that broadened, changed or even was directly contrary to the Council's provisions. Since I knew precisely the entire proceeding of the Council, from the often very lengthy discussions...up to the repeated votes leading to the final formulations, as well as the texts that included the precise regulations for the implementation of the desired reform, you can imagine my amazement, my growing displeasure, indeed my indignation, especially regarding specific contradictions and changes that would necessarily have lasting consequences.

Cardinal Stickler spends the rest of his recollections of his time as a conciliar *peritus* detailing particular examples of

Sacred Then and Sacred Now

what he considers the new liturgy's departure from agreed-upon norms at the Council.[43]

"The Tridentine Mass isn't so ancient–it dates back only to the Council of Trent."

The Council of Trent did not create the traditional Latin Mass (now known as the extraordinary form of the Roman rite) from scratch. The idea of doing such a thing would not have occurred to anyone. It merely codified an already-existing liturgy. In all essentials, the Roman Missal of 1570–the so-called Tridentine missal–is identical to the Roman Missal of 1474. That missal is likewise all but identical to what preceded it. As Dom David Knowles explained in 1971:

> The missal of 1570 was indeed the result of instructions given at Trent, but it was, in fact, as regards the Ordinary, Canon, Proper of the time and much else a replica of the Roman missal of 1474, which in its turn repeated in all essentials the practice of the Roman Church of the epoch of Innocent III, which itself derived from the usage of Gregory the Great and his successors in the seventh century. In short the missal of 1570 was in essentials the usage of the mainstream of medieval European Liturgy.... The missal of 1570 was essentially traditional, far more so than the new missal of today.[44]

Even if we should suddenly discover a collection of ancient liturgical prayers, it does not follow that they should be incorporated into the Mass. The abrupt insertion of additional texts, whatever their alleged antiquity, on the grounds that they would make the resulting Mass more "traditional," would violate the traditional manner of liturgical development whereby changes are made gradually and imperceptibly over centuries and grow organically from forms already existing (as Vatican II put it).

Pope Pius XII spoke impatiently of those who "are bent on the restoration of all the ancient rites and ceremonies indiscriminately." "The liturgy of the early ages is most cer-

Common Misconceptions

tainly worthy of all veneration," the Pope observed. But

> ancient usage must not be esteemed more suitable and proper, either in its own right or in its significance for later times and new situations, on the simple ground that it carries the savor and aroma of antiquity. The more recent liturgical rites likewise deserve reverence and respect. They, too, owe their inspiration to the Holy Spirit, who assists the Church in every age even to the consummation of the world. They are equally the resources used by the majestic Spouse of Jesus Christ to promote and procure the sanctity of man.[45]

In fact, any sudden or dramatic change to the liturgy is unwise in and of itself, for the reasons the future John Henry Cardinal Newman outlined in 1831:

> Granting that the forms [of the liturgy] are not immediately from God, still long use has made them divine *to us*; for the spirit of religion has so penetrated and quickened them, that to destroy them is, in respect to the multitude of men, to unsettle and dislodge the religious principle itself. In most minds usage has so identified them with the notion of religion, that the one cannot be extirpated without the other. Their faith will not bear transplanting....

> The services and ordinances of the Church are the outward form in which religion has been for ages represented to the world, and has ever been known to us. Places consecrated to God's honor, clergy carefully set apart for His service, the Lord's day piously observed, the public forms of prayer, the decencies of worship, these things viewed as a whole, are *sacred* relatively to us, even if they were not, as they are, divinely sanctioned. Rites which the Church has appointed...being long used cannot be disused without harm to our souls.[46]

And that, among other reasons, is why Pope Benedict, the Church's chief physician, was so concerned to dress this great wound by restoring the classical Roman liturgy to its rightful place in the Catholic world.

Sacred Then and Sacred Now

1. Pius XI, Apostolic Letter *Officiorum Omnium*, cited in John XXIII, Apostolic Constitution *Veterum Sapientia*.
2. Pius XII, *Musicae Sacrae* 44, 45.
3. *Sacrosanctum Concilium* 36.
4. *Sacrosanctum Concilium* 54.
5. Michael J. Miller, "The International and the Introibo: How the Catholic Mass Converted a Communist," *Sursum Corda*, Winter 1999.
6. Barbara Kay, "Latin's Second Coming," *National Post* [Canada], October 18, 2006.
7. Ibid.
8. Michael Davies, ed., *The Wisdom of Adrian Fortescue* (Fort Collins, Colo.: Roman Catholic Books, 1999), 146.
9. Cardinal Alfons Stickler, "Recollections of a Vatican II Peritus," *The Latin Mass*, Winter 1999.
10. Ibid.
11. Scott M.P. Reid, ed., *A Bitter Trial: Evelyn Waugh and John Carmel Cardinal Heenan on the Liturgical Changes* (London: St. Austin Press, 1996).
12. Cardinal Edward Egan, "Room for All," *Catholic New York*, July 19, 2007.
13. Peter A. Huff, *Allen Tate and the Catholic Revival: Trace of the Fugitive Gods* (New York: Paulist, 1996), 23.
14. Michael P. Foley, "From Active to Activist: The Kidnapping of Active Participation," *The Latin Mass*, Spring 2007, 25.
15. Ibid., 24.
16. Reid, ed., *A Bitter Trial*.
17. Monsignor Richard J. Schuler, "'Active Participation' in the Church's Liturgy: What Did the Second Vatican Council Mean?" *Adoremus Bulletin*, October 1996.
18. Quoted in Foley, "From Active to Activist," 25.
19. Ibid.
20. Kenneth Myers, "A New Look at the Old Mass," *Homiletic & Pastoral Review*, March 2007, 50.
21. Stickler, "Recollections of a Vatican II Peritus."
22. Cardinal Joseph Ratzinger, *The Feast of Faith: Approaches to a Theology of the Liturgy*, trans. Graham Harrison (San Francisco: Ignatius Press, 1986), 89.
23. Cardinal Joseph Ratzinger, *The Spirit of the Liturgy*, trans. John Saward (San Francisco: Ignatius Press, 2000), 171-75. Emphasis in original.
24. Ibid., 94.
25. Alcuin Reid, ed., *Looking Again at the Question of the Liturgy with Cardinal Ratzinger: Proceedings of the July 2001 Fontgombault Liturgical Conference* (Farnborough, Hants [U.K.]: St. Augustine's Press, 2004), 151.

Common Misconceptions

26. U.M. Lang, *Turning Towards the Lord: Orientation in Liturgical Prayer* (San Francisco: Ignatius Press, 2004), 43-46.
27. Monsignor Klaus Gamber, *The Reform of the Roman Liturgy: Its Problems and Background*, trans. Klaus D. Grimm (Fort Collins, Colo.: Foundation for Catholic Reform, 1993), 152, 165.
28. Quoted in Lang, *Turning Towards the Lord*, 28.
29. Ratzinger, *Spirit of the Liturgy*, 70.
30. Cardinal Joseph Ratzinger, "Foreword," in Lang, *Turning Towards the Lord*, 11.
31. Lang mentions such examples as "the sun of righteousness (Mal. 4:2), the feet of the Lord standing on the Mount of Olives, which lies before Jerusalem on the east (Zech. 14:4), the day dawning from on high (Lk. 1:78), the angel ascending from the rising of the sun with the seal of the living God (Rev. 7:2), not to mention the Johannine light imagery." Lang, *Turning Towards the Lord*, 41.
32. Lang, *Turning Towards the Lord*, 100.
33. Ibid., 41.
34. Ibid., 109-110.
35. http://sacramentary.blogspot.com/2007/07/exclusive-interview-with-fr-joseph.html (accessed August 6, 2007).
36. Ratzinger, "Foreword," 11.
37. Gamber, *The Reform of the Roman Liturgy*, 61.
38. Gianni Cardinale, "Nova et vetera: Interview with Cardinal Darío Castrillón Hoyos," *30 Days*, June/July 2007.
39. Alcuin Reid, "*Sacrosanctum Concilium* and the Organic Development of the Liturgy," *The Latin Mass*, Spring 2007, 11.
40. Ibid.
41. Ibid.
42. Ibid.
43. As of this printing, this writer's English translation of Cardinal Stickler's memoir is available at http://www.latinmassmagazine.com/vatican_ii_peritus.asp.
44. Alcuin Reid, O.S.B., *The Organic Development of the Liturgy* (Farnborough, Hants [U.K.]: Saint Michael's Abbey Press, 2004), 34 and n101.
45. Pius XII, *Mediator Dei* 61.
46. John Henry Newman, Sermon on the Feast of the Circumcision of the Lord, *Parochial and Plain Sermons*, vol. II, 75, 77-78; quoted in Reid, *Organic Development*, 57.

Appendix A

Pope Benedict XVI's Letter to Bishops

July 7, 2007

My dear Brother Bishops,

With great trust and hope, I am consigning to you as Pastors the text of a new Apostolic Letter "Motu Proprio data" on the use of the Roman liturgy prior to the reform of 1970. The document is the fruit of much reflection, numerous consultations and prayer.

News reports and judgments made without sufficient information have created no little confusion. There have been very divergent reactions ranging from joyful acceptance to harsh opposition, about a plan whose contents were in reality unknown.

This document was most directly opposed on account of two fears, which I would like to address somewhat more closely in this letter.

In the first place, there is the fear that the document detracts from the authority of the Second Vatican Council, one of whose essential decisions–the liturgical reform–is being called into question. This fear is unfounded. In this regard, it must first be said that the Missal published by Paul VI and then republished in two subsequent editions by John Paul II, obviously is and continues to be the normal Form–the

Sacred Then and Sacred Now

Forma ordinaria–of the Eucharistic Liturgy. The last version of the *Missale Romanum* prior to the Council, which was published with the authority of Pope John XXIII in 1962 and used during the Council, will now be able to be used as a *Forma extraordinaria* of the liturgical celebration. It is not appropriate to speak of these two versions of the Roman Missal as if they were "two Rites." Rather, it is a matter of a twofold use of one and the same rite.

As for the use of the 1962 Missal as a *Forma extraordinaria* of the liturgy of the Mass, I would like to draw attention to the fact that this Missal was never juridically abrogated and, consequently, in principle, was always permitted. At the time of the introduction of the new Missal, it did not seem necessary to issue specific norms for the possible use of the earlier Missal. Probably it was thought that it would be a matter of a few individual cases which would be resolved, case by case, on the local level.

Afterwards, however, it soon became apparent that a good number of people remained strongly attached to this usage of the Roman rite, which had been familiar to them from childhood. This was especially the case in countries where the liturgical movement had provided many people with a notable liturgical formation and a deep, personal familiarity with the earlier Form of the liturgical celebration. We all know that, in the movement led by Archbishop Lefebvre, fidelity to the old Missal became an external mark of identity; the reasons for the break which arose over this, however, were at a deeper level. Many people who clearly accepted the binding character of the Second Vatican Council, and were faithful to the Pope and the Bishops, nonetheless also desired to recover the form of the sacred liturgy that was dear to them. This occurred above all because in many places celebrations were not faithful to the prescriptions of the new Missal, but

Pope Benedict XVI's Letter to Bishops

the latter actually was understood as authorizing or even requiring creativity, which frequently led to deformations of the liturgy which were hard to bear. I am speaking from experience, since I too lived through that period with all its hopes and its confusion. And I have seen how arbitrary deformations of the liturgy caused deep pain to individuals totally rooted in the faith of the Church.

Pope John Paul II thus felt obliged to provide, in his *motu proprio Ecclesia Dei* (2 July 1988), guidelines for the use of the 1962 Missal; that document, however, did not contain detailed prescriptions but appealed in a general way to the generous response of Bishops towards the "legitimate aspirations" of those members of the faithful who requested this usage of the Roman rite. At the time, the Pope primarily wanted to assist the Society of Saint Pius X to recover full unity with the Successor of Peter, and sought to heal a wound experienced ever more painfully. Unfortunately this reconciliation has not yet come about. Nonetheless, a number of communities have gratefully made use of the possibilities provided by the *motu proprio*. On the other hand, difficulties remain concerning the use of the 1962 Missal outside of these groups, because of the lack of precise juridical norms, particularly because Bishops, in such cases, frequently feared that the authority of the Council would be called into question. Immediately after the Second Vatican Council it was presumed that requests for the use of the 1962 Missal would be limited to the older generation which had grown up with it, but in the meantime it has clearly been demonstrated that young persons too have discovered this liturgical form, felt its attraction and found in it a form of encounter with the Mystery of the Most Holy Eucharist, particularly suited to them. Thus the need has arisen for a clearer juridical regulation which had not been foreseen at the time of the 1988 *motu proprio*. The present Norms are also meant to free Bishops from constantly having to evaluate anew how they are to respond to various situations.

In the second place, the fear was expressed in discussions about the awaited *motu proprio* that the possibility of a wider use of the 1962 Missal would lead to disarray or even divisions within parish communities. This fear also strikes me as quite unfounded. The use of the old Missal presupposes a certain degree of liturgical formation and some knowledge of the Latin language; neither of these is found very often. Already from these concrete presuppositions, it is clearly seen that the new Missal will certainly remain the ordinary Form of the Roman rite, not only on account of the juridical norms, but also because of the actual situation of the communities of the faithful.

It is true that there have been exaggerations and at times social aspects unduly linked to the attitude of the faithful attached to the ancient Latin liturgical tradition. Your charity and pastoral prudence will be an incentive and guide for improving these. For that matter, the two Forms of the usage of the Roman rite can be mutually enriching: new Saints and some of the new Prefaces can and should be inserted in the old Missal. The *"Ecclesia Dei"* Commission, in contact with various bodies devoted to the *usus antiquior*, will study the practical possibilities in this regard. The celebration of the Mass according to the Missal of Paul VI will be able to demonstrate, more powerfully than has been the case hitherto, the sacrality which attracts many people to the former usage. The most sure guarantee that the Missal of Paul VI can unite parish communities and be loved by them consists in its being celebrated with great reverence in harmony with the liturgical directives. This will bring out the spiritual richness and the theological depth of this Missal.

I now come to the positive reason which motivated my

Pope Benedict XVI's Letter to Bishops

decision to issue this *motu proprio* updating that of 1988. It is a matter of coming to an interior reconciliation in the heart of the Church. Looking back over the past, to the divisions which in the course of the centuries have rent the Body of Christ, one continually has the impression that, at critical moments when divisions were coming about, not enough was done by the Church's leaders to maintain or regain reconciliation and unity. One has the impression that omissions on the part of the Church have had their share of blame for the fact that these divisions were able to harden. This glance at the past imposes an obligation on us today: to make every effort to enable for all those who truly desire unity to remain in that unity or to attain it anew. I think of a sentence in the Second Letter to the Corinthians, where Paul writes: "Our mouth is open to you, Corinthians; our heart is wide. You are not restricted by us, but you are restricted in your own affections. In return...widen your hearts also!" (*2 Cor* 6:11-13). Paul was certainly speaking in another context, but his exhortation can and must touch us too, precisely on this subject. Let us generously open our hearts and make room for everything that the faith itself allows.

There is no contradiction between the two editions of the Roman Missal. In the history of the liturgy there is growth and progress, but no rupture. What earlier generations held as sacred, remains sacred and great for us too, and it cannot be all of a sudden entirely forbidden or even considered harmful. It behooves all of us to preserve the riches which have developed in the Church's faith and prayer, and to give them their proper place. Needless to say, in order to experience full communion, the priests of the communities adhering to the former usage cannot, as a matter of principle, exclude celebrating according to the new books. The total exclusion of the new rite would not in fact be consistent with the recognition of its value and holiness.

Sacred Then and Sacred Now

In conclusion, dear Brothers, I very much wish to stress that these new norms do not in any way lessen your own authority and responsibility, either for the liturgy or for the pastoral care of your faithful. Each Bishop, in fact, is the moderator of the liturgy in his own Diocese (cf. *Sacrosanctum Concilium*, 22: "Sacrae Liturgiae moderatio ab Ecclesiae auctoritate unice pendet quae quidem est apud Apostolicam Sedem et, ad normam iuris, apud Episcopum").

Nothing is taken away, then, from the authority of the Bishop, whose role remains that of being watchful that all is done in peace and serenity. Should some problem arise which the parish priest cannot resolve, the local Ordinary will always be able to intervene, in full harmony, however, with all that has been laid down by the new norms of the *motu proprio*.

Furthermore, I invite you, dear Brothers, to send to the Holy See an account of your experiences, three years after this *motu proprio* has taken effect. If truly serious difficulties come to light, ways to remedy them can be sought.

Dear Brothers, with gratitude and trust, I entrust to your hearts as Pastors these pages and the norms of the *motu proprio*. Let us always be mindful of the words of the Apostle Paul addressed to the presbyters of Ephesus: "Take heed to yourselves and to all the flock, in which the Holy Spirit has made you overseers, to care for the Church of God which he obtained with the blood of his own Son" (*Acts* 20:28).

I entrust these norms to the powerful intercession of Mary, Mother of the Church, and I cordially impart my Apostolic Blessing to you, dear Brothers, to the parish priests of your dioceses, and to all the priests, your co-workers, as well as to all your faithful.

Given at Saint Peter's, 7 July 2007.

BENEDICTUS PP. XVI

Appendix B

The *motu proprio* *Summorum Pontificum*

Up to our own times, it has been the constant concern of supreme pontiffs to ensure that the Church of Christ offers a worthy ritual to the Divine Majesty, "to the praise and glory of His name," and "to the benefit of all His Holy Church."

Since time immemorial it has been necessary–as it is also for the future–to maintain the principle according to which "each particular Church must concur with the universal Church, not only as regards the doctrine of the faith and the sacramental signs, but also as regards the usages universally accepted by uninterrupted apostolic tradition, which must be observed not only to avoid errors but also to transmit the integrity of the faith, because the Church's law of prayer corresponds to her law of faith."[1]

Among the pontiffs who showed that requisite concern, particularly outstanding is the name of St. Gregory the Great, who made every effort to ensure that the new peoples of Europe received both the Catholic faith and the treasures of worship and culture that had been accumulated by the Romans in preceding centuries. He commanded that the form of the sacred liturgy as celebrated in Rome (concerning both the Sacrifice of Mass and the Divine Office) be conserved. He took great care to ensure the dissemination of monks and

Sacred Then and Sacred Now

nuns who, following the Rule of St. Benedict, together with the announcement of the Gospel illustrated with their lives the wise provision of their Rule that "nothing should be placed before the work of God." In this way the sacred liturgy, celebrated according to the Roman use, enriched not only the faith and piety but also the culture of many peoples. It is known, in fact, that the Latin liturgy of the Church in its various forms, in each century of the Christian era, has been a spur to the spiritual life of many saints, has reinforced many peoples in the virtue of religion and enriched their piety.

Many other Roman pontiffs, in the course of the centuries, showed particular solicitude in ensuring that the sacred liturgy accomplished this task more effectively. Outstanding among them is St. Pius V who, sustained by great pastoral zeal and following the exhortations of the Council of Trent, renewed the entire liturgy of the Church, oversaw the publication of liturgical books amended and "renewed in accordance with the norms of the Fathers," and provided them for the use of the Latin Church.

One of the liturgical books of the Roman rite is the Roman Missal, which developed in the city of Rome and, with the passing of the centuries, little by little took forms very similar to that it has had in recent times.

"It was towards this same goal that succeeding Roman Pontiffs directed their energies during the subsequent centuries in order to ensure that the rites and liturgical books were brought up to date and when necessary clarified. From the beginning of this century they undertook a more general reform."[2] Thus our predecessors Clement VIII, Urban VIII, St. Pius X,[3] Benedict XV, Pius XII and Blessed John XXIII all played a part.

In more recent times, Vatican Council II expressed a desire that the respectful reverence due to divine worship

The motu proprio Summorum Pontificum

should be renewed and adapted to the needs of our time. Moved by this desire our predecessor, the Supreme Pontiff Paul VI, approved, in 1970, reformed and partly renewed liturgical books for the Latin Church. These, translated into the various languages of the world, were willingly accepted by bishops, priests and faithful. John Paul II amended the third typical edition of the Roman Missal. Thus Roman pontiffs have operated to ensure that "this kind of liturgical edifice...should again appear resplendent for its dignity and harmony."[4]

But in some regions, no small numbers of faithful adhered and continue to adhere with great love and affection to the earlier liturgical forms. These had so deeply marked their culture and their spirit that in 1984 the Supreme Pontiff John Paul II, moved by a concern for the pastoral care of these faithful, with the special indult *Quattuor abhinc annos*, issued by the Congregation for Divine Worship, granted permission to use the Roman Missal published by Blessed John XXIII in the year 1962. Later, in the year 1988, John Paul II with the Apostolic Letter given as *motu proprio*, *Ecclesia Dei*, exhorted bishops to make generous use of this power in favor of all the faithful who so desired.

Following the insistent prayers of these faithful, long deliberated upon by our predecessor John Paul II, and after having listened to the views of the Cardinal Fathers of the Consistory of 22 March 2006, having reflected deeply upon all aspects of the question, invoked the Holy Spirit and trusting in the help of God, with these Apostolic Letters we establish the following:

Art 1. The Roman Missal promulgated by Paul VI is the ordinary expression of the *Lex orandi* (Law of prayer) of the Catholic Church of the Latin rite. Nonetheless, the Roman Missal promulgated by St. Pius V and reissued by Bl. John

Sacred Then and Sacred Now

XXIII is to be considered as an extraordinary expression of that same *Lex orandi*, and must be given due honor for its venerable and ancient usage. These two expressions of the Church's *Lex orandi* will in no way lead to a division in the Church's *Lex credendi* (Law of belief). They are, in fact, two usages of the one Roman rite.

It is, therefore, permissible to celebrate the Sacrifice of the Mass following the typical edition of the Roman Missal promulgated by Bl. John XXIII in 1962 and never abrogated, as an extraordinary form of the Liturgy of the Church. The conditions for the use of this Missal as laid down by earlier documents *Quattuor abhinc annos* and *Ecclesia Dei*, are substituted as follows:

Art. 2. In Masses celebrated without the people, each Catholic priest of the Latin rite, whether secular or regular, may use the Roman Missal published by Bl. Pope John XXIII in 1962, or the Roman Missal promulgated by Pope Paul VI in 1970, and may do so on any day with the exception of the Easter Triduum. For such celebrations, with either one Missal or the other, the priest has no need for permission from the Apostolic See or from his Ordinary.

Art. 3. Communities of Institutes of consecrated life and of Societies of apostolic life, of either pontifical or diocesan right, wishing to celebrate Mass in accordance with the edition of the Roman Missal promulgated in 1962, for conventual or "community" celebration in their oratories, may do so. If an individual community or an entire Institute or Society wishes to undertake such celebrations often, habitually or permanently, the decision must be taken by the Superiors Major, in accordance with the law and following their own specific decrees and statutes.

Art. 4. Celebrations of Mass as mentioned above in art. 2 may—observing all the norms of law—also be attended by faithful who, of their own free will, ask to be admitted.

The motu proprio Summorum Pontificum

Art. 5. § 1 In parishes, where there is a stable group of faithful who adhere to the earlier liturgical tradition, the pastor should willingly accept their requests to celebrate the Mass according to the rite of the Roman Missal published in 1962, and ensure that the welfare of these faithful harmonizes with the ordinary pastoral care of the parish, under the guidance of the bishop in accordance with canon 392, avoiding discord and favoring the unity of the whole Church.

§ 2 Celebration in accordance with the Missal of Bl. John XXIII may take place on working days; while on Sundays and feast days one such celebration may also be held.

§ 3 For faithful and priests who request it, the pastor should also allow celebrations in this extraordinary form for special circumstances such as marriages, funerals or occasional celebrations, e.g. pilgrimages.

§ 4 Priests who use the Missal of Bl. John XXIII must be qualified to do so and not juridically impeded.

§ 5 In churches that are not parish or conventual churches, it is the duty of the Rector of the church to grant the above permission.

Art. 6. In Masses celebrated in the presence of the people in accordance with the Missal of Bl. John XXIII, the readings may be given in the vernacular, using editions recognized by the Apostolic See.

Art. 7. If a group of lay faithful, as mentioned in art. 5 § 1, has not obtained satisfaction to their requests from the pastor, they should inform the diocesan bishop. The bishop is strongly requested to satisfy their wishes. If he cannot arrange for such celebration to take place, the matter should be referred to the Pontifical Commission "Ecclesia Dei."

Art. 8. A bishop who, desirous of satisfying such requests, but who for various reasons is unable to do so, may refer the

Sacred Then and Sacred Now

problem to the Commission "Ecclesia Dei" to obtain counsel and assistance.

Art. 9. § 1 The pastor, having attentively examined all aspects, may also grant permission to use the earlier ritual for the administration of the Sacraments of Baptism, Marriage, Penance, and the Anointing of the Sick, if the good of souls would seem to require it.

§ 2 Ordinaries are given the right to celebrate the Sacrament of Confirmation using the earlier Roman Pontifical, if the good of souls would seem to require it.

§ 3 Clerics ordained "in sacris constitutis" may use the Roman Breviary promulgated by Bl. John XXIII in 1962.

Art. 10. The ordinary of a particular place, if he feels it appropriate, may erect a personal parish in accordance with can. 518 for celebrations following the ancient form of the Roman rite, or appoint a chaplain, while observing all the norms of law.

Art. 11. The Pontifical Commission "Ecclesia Dei," erected by John Paul II in 1988,[5] continues to exercise its function. Said Commission will have the form, duties and norms that the Roman Pontiff wishes to assign it.

Art. 12. This Commission, apart from the powers it enjoys, will exercise the authority of the Holy See, supervising the observance and application of these dispositions.

We order that everything We have *established with these* Apostolic Letters issued as *Motu Proprio* be considered as "established and decreed," and to be observed from 14 September of this year, Feast of the Exaltation of the Cross, whatever there may be to the contrary.

From Rome, at St. Peter's, 7 July 2007, third year of Our Pontificate.

BENEDICT XVI

The motu proprio Summorum Pontificum

1. General Instruction of the Roman Missal, 3rd ed., 2002, no. 397.
2. John Paul II, Apostolic Letter *Vicesimus quintus annus*, 4 December 1988, 3: AAS 81 (1989), 899.
3. Ibid.
4. St. Pius X, Apostolic Letter *motu propio data, Abhinc duos annos*, 23 October 1913: AAS 5 (1913), 449-450; cf. John Paul II, Apostolic Letter *Vicesimus quintus annus*, no. 3: AAS 81 (1989), 899.
5. Cf. John Paul II, Apostolic Letter *motu proprio data, Ecclesia Dei*, 2 July 1988, 6: AAS 80 (1988), 1498.

Appendix C

Useful Resources

More and more resources are becoming available for those interested in the extraordinary form of the Mass. Here are a few of the truly essential ones.

Liturgical Resources

Sancta Missa, http://www.sanctamissa.org

A beautiful site containing invaluable training resources for priests, including an online tutorial with video, and the entire 1962 Missal in .pdf form. Instructions for altar servers are also available.

Musica Sacra, http://www.musicasacra.com

This is the website of the Church Music Association of America. The entire *Graduale Romanum* (1961) and *Liber Usualis* (1961), two important collections of Gregorian chant, are available online for free. You can also learn about Gregorian chant and how to read chant notation.

Latin

It is unnecessary to know a single word of Latin in order to follow the extraordinary form with ease. Still, should you wish to learn this sacred language, you can find a free online course at the website of the Latin Mass Society of England and Wales:

http://www.latin-mass-society.org/simplicissimus/index.htm

Sacred Then and Sacred Now

An audio pronunciation guide to the Latin of the Mass is available at the website of the Latin Mass Society of Ireland: **http://www.latinmassireland.org/thelatinmass/latinmass_audio.html**

Many other useful Latin resources, from learning aids to pronunciation guides, are available at the Una Voce America website: **http://www.unavoce.org/latin.htm**

News and Information

New Liturgical Movement, http://newliturgicalmovement.blogspot.com

An interesting and informative blog that discusses all manner of liturgical subjects. You will learn a great deal by reading the various items posted there on a daily basis, as well as the useful discussions that invariably ensue.

Summorum Pontificum, http://www.summorumpontificum.net

A useful site that contains news and other items of interest pertaining to the implementation of the *motu proprio*. It also features an archive containing reactions by various bishops around the world.

Videos, Books, and Missals

Roman Catholic Books, http://www.booksforcatholics.com

Reprints important Catholic classics, and offers altar missals and laymen's hand missals for sale.

The Most Beautiful Thing This Side of Heaven

This 52-minute DVD, which comes with two helpful booklets, explains how to offer the extraordinary form of the Mass. (The video depicts a Low Mass.)

Useful Resources

The Reform of the Roman Liturgy: Its Problems and Background, by Msgr. Klaus Gamber. Highly recommended by Cardinal Ratzinger when it first appeared, this book by the eminent Msgr. Gamber is important for laymen seeking to understand the true history and consequences of the liturgical reform.

Iota Unum: A Study of the Changes in the Catholic Church in the 20th Century, by Romano Amerio. In 2005, the important Jesuit newspaper *La Civiltà Cattolica* spoke highly of "Amerio's intellectual and moral stature," and of "the importance of his philosophical-theological vision for the contemporary Church."

Cranmer's Godly Order, by Michael Davies. The late Michael Davies was beautifully eulogized by Cardinal Ratzinger in 2004. This book, the first in Davies' *Liturgical Revolution* trilogy, chronicles the reform of the liturgy in sixteenth-century England. The other volumes in the trilogy are *Pope John's Council* and *Pope Paul's New Mass*.

The Heresy of Formlessness: The Roman Liturgy and Its Enemies, by Martin Mosebach. In this book Martin Mosebach–winner of the Georg Buechner prize, the highest German literary award–produced one of the most important and beautifully written defenses of the extraordinary form that has appeared in any language.

Appendix D

Sermon of Father Calvin Goodwin, FSSP

September 14, 2007

On September 14, 2007, for the first time in the network's history, EWTN televised a Solemn High Mass in the extraordinary form from its shrine in Hanceville, Alabama. Father Calvin Goodwin, who preached on that day, took this historic moment to describe the significance of Pope Benedict's motu proprio, and the excellence of the Church's traditional liturgy.*

The Priestly Fraternity of St. Peter, whom you see in the sanctuary today, would like to thank Mother Angelica, Mother Vicar and the Poor Clare community for their gracious invitation to celebrate this Mass here today in this magnificent church. We are particularly grateful to Bishop Foley of the Diocese of Birmingham for supporting our presence here today, as well as to the members of the EWTN staff and to the board of directors of this tremendous enterprise, born of Mother Angelica's faith and wisdom and which has been so fruitful for the needs of the Church all around the world for a quarter of a century.

---

*On the same day, at the Shrine of Loreto, the Holy Father's emissary, Cardinal Darío Castrillón Hoyos, celebrated a Pontifical High Mass using the old Latin Missal. (The actual edition he used was published by Roman Catholic Books, and is still available from RCB, BooksforCatholics.com; Box 2286, Fort Collins, CO 80524.)

Sacred Then and Sacred Now

There are so many things that could be said on this momentous occasion of the coming into full legal power in the Church of the Holy Father's *motu proprio* on the traditional Mass. I will do no more than offer a few reflections, as the least of the members of the Priestly Fraternity of St. Peter. There are many who would be able to offer more eloquent and apposite thoughts. My comments reflect only my own poor grasp of the gift that the successor of Peter offers to the Church in his teaching and his decrees in the *motu proprio Summorum Pontificum*.

Today marks a great moment in the Church in modern times. This Mass offered today for the needs and intentions of our Holy Father, Benedict XVI, is a concrete and visible token of that interior reconciliation within the Church that the Holy Father has both called for and made possible through his recent *motu proprio*, which restores the traditional liturgical rites to a central place at the heart of the Church's life.

Certainly no one now is unaware of the painful confusions and divisions which afflicted the Church's interior life in recent years. The Supreme Pontiff bears poignant witness to these afflictions when in the letter to the universal episcopate, which accompanied the *motu proprio*, he writes, "I am speaking from experience, since I too lived through that period, with all its hopes and its confusion. And I have seen how arbitrary deformations of the liturgy caused deep pain to individuals totally rooted in the faith of the Church." And so the Vicar of Christ, making use of that personal authority which binds the universal Church and which is his alone, has determined that healing of those painful wounds must begin—and that it must begin at the heart of the Church, in the sanctuary, in the Holy Sacrifice which makes present on the altar that very exaltation of the saving Passion of Christ which is commemorated in the Feast which we celebrate here today.

So, therefore, let any spirit of suspicion which has led to division among Catholics be banished once and for all by this proclamation of the Vicar of Christ, in which he says, "What earlier generations held as sacred, remains sacred and great for us too, and it cannot be all of a sudden entirely forbidden or even considered harmful." And we cannot fail to note that the ancient feast which we celebrate today bears witness to the fact that out of the most abject suffering the world has ever witnessed—the ignominious Passion and death on the Cross of the Son of God—there emanated reason for joy and exultation, a joy and exultation that will endure as long as this world endures and indeed is crowned for all eternity in heaven. So too, though the Church has witnessed contradictions and conflicts throughout her history, she, the unspotted Bride of Christ, always emerges intact to continue her mission for the honor of God and the needs of souls. Out of this conviction, the Vicar of Christ offers to the whole Church an invitation to what he calls an interior reconciliation much needed and long awaited and so deeply appreciated by faithful Catholics everywhere.

Still, it is not sufficient to take advantage only of the joy of this great moment. We must apply ourselves to the task of appreciating more fully the substance of the mind of the Church as articulated by the Successor of Peter. What, then, does the Holy Father have in mind as he restores the immemorial rite of the Mass, with all the liturgical rites and uses of the Latin Rite? What does he expect it to achieve in the life of the Church?

Sacred Then and Sacred Now

Without attempting to speak for him, let us briefly look at the rite itself, so as to glean from its nature and character what it is that the Supreme Pontiff wishes to offer through its restoration to the attention of the whole Church. Certainly we will find, in the rite itself, elements revelatory of the essence of authentic Catholic liturgy. For as Pope John Paul II of blessed memory reminded us just a very few years ago, "In the Roman Missal so-called of St. Pius V, one finds the most beautiful prayers, with which the priest expresses the deepest sense of humility and reverence before the Sacred Mysteries. These reveal the very substance of what liturgy is."

No doubt much of the ceremony of today's Mass will be unfamiliar to many. Two things in particular will probably stand out. One is that the Mass is celebrated entirely in Latin. The other is that for much of the ceremony, the priest-celebrant prays facing the altar. These phenomena are by no means the only significant ones, but they are both immediately different from what many have become accustomed to in the liturgy as most often celebrated in recent times.

Yet these phenomena, however much they may bring with them the shock of the unfamiliar, are nonetheless integral to the most central principles of liturgical prayer in the Catholic Church. And they are hallowed by an unbroken tradition—which, as the Council of Trent solemnly defined, is rooted in the liturgy of apostolic times. Still, given the more common liturgical practice of recent times, it should cause no surprise if good and sincere people simply ask, "Why is the Mass in a language that I don't understand, and the rites in a configuration that makes it impossible for me to see what's going on?"

Sermon of Father Calvin Goodwin, FSSP

It should be made clear, then: this venerable rite of Holy Mass in no way has as its goal the obscuring of the elements of the Mass. Just the opposite. It is so constructed as to be eminently revelatory, as Pope John Paul said, of the very substance of what liturgy is. There is no need, nor would it be germane to the context of a sermon, to analyze elements that may have contributed to certain confusions and anomalies during a time of tumultuous changes in the Church's life. For his part, and this is surely sufficient for us, Pope Benedict XVI clearly comprehends the historical context and does not forbear to draw certain difficult but unavoidable conclusions when he says, "In many places celebrations were not faithful to the prescriptions of the new Missal, but the latter actually was understood as authorizing or even requiring creativity, which frequently led to deformations of the liturgy which were hard to bear." Beyond that, it is surely our priority to note first the profound compassion with which the Vicar of Christ seeks to bind up the wounds of those who have suffered, and then the sober and insistent fashion in which he summons the whole Church, bishops, priests and faithful, to that interior reconciliation without which our service of God, liturgically and otherwise, would be gravely impaired.

All the varied rites of the Church stand together in offering to God the same worship which His human creatures owe to Him, and all these rites, singly and together, are equally bound constantly to reflect upon the fidelity and constancy with which they do so. The texts of today's Mass–today's Feast–reveal to us a great deal about the essence of liturgical prayer. In the Introit we read, "May God have mercy on us and bless us. May He cause the light of His countenance to shine upon us." What do we

Sacred Then and Sacred Now

perceive here, if not the reality that in this world we are threatened by a darkness, a darkness founded in elements of sin and error? We perceive further an acknowledgment that it is God's merciful action that we must await to effect the dispelling of that darkness.

In the Gospel, we read just how that darkness is dispelled. It is through Christ alone—Christ our Light—and it is Christ Himself Who guides us by the light of truth, that light which saves. "Whilst you have the light, believe in the light, that you may be Children of Light." What is our response to the action of God Who saves us in Christ the Eternal Light? It must be to believe in that Light. Thus in Holy Mass, everything builds on that belief in the Light. But—and this should lead us to profound reflection—the initiative is God's. And Christ alone is, in the Incarnation, the means of that initiative.

Just a few days ago, the Holy Father gave an allocution in Germany in which he reflected upon the essential elements of Catholic liturgical prayer. "In all our efforts on behalf of the liturgy," he said, "the determining factor must always be our looking to God. We stand before God. He speaks to us first, and then we speak to Him. I ask you to celebrate the sacred liturgy with your gaze fixed upon God within the communion of saints, the living Church of every place and time."

The liturgical prayer of the Church is, therefore, first of all something given to us by God, something which we receive, something to which we are obliged faithfully and humbly to conform ourselves. What is obscure in a world so convinced of its self-sufficiency is made plain to the eyes of faith, turned and lifted toward Him. It is given and revealed to us in fact by God, through an unbroken tradition of rites, which embody that

Sermon of Father Calvin Goodwin, FSSP

Tradition that stretches back directly to the Apostles themselves. The world's cultural inclinations and fashions pass and fade away, but the Light remains constant.

The ancient character of the Church's liturgical actions—their words, gestures and ceremonies—reflect this enduring Light in a concrete and sensible way. The words pronounced at the altar today, as well as the very gestures and motions employed, are to a very significant degree the same words, gestures and motions as those used by Blessed John XXIII and by St. Pius V, by St. John Vianney and St. Dominic, by St. Miguel Pro and St. Edmund Campion, by the martyrs of North America and the martyrs of the Crusades, by St. Maximilian Kolbe and St. Augustine of Hippo—hallowed words, hallowed gestures, hallowed action, hallowed not only by use but by where they come from, that precious and holy Tradition that has sanctified individuals, made devout families, given abundant vocations and martyrs to the Church and to the honor of God for almost two millennia.

As the Holy Father states in *Summorum Pontificum*, "It is evident that the Latin liturgy has stimulated in the spiritual life of very many saints in every century of the Christian age and strengthened in the virtue of religion so many peoples and made fertile their piety." You know that in the churches of the Eastern rites there is a wall, beautifully decorated, called the *iconostasis*, which separates the gaze of the people from what is transpiring in the sanctuary. In the ancient times of the Church, when the most central part of the Mass was to begin, a curtain used to be drawn across the sanctuary, in order to withhold from profane gaze the sacred Mysteries.

No longer is such a curtain drawn. It is not needed, because God in the Holy Ghost has guided the Church to that same reality—the reality represented in the Eastern Church by the *iconostasis*—with a sacred language, a non-everyday special language devoted only to the Church's most holy endeavors. It serves as a verbal curtain drawn over the Mysteries being carried out at the altar to remind us that, yes, there is a wide and fathomless gap between the incomprehensible majesty and holiness of God, on the one hand, and our human sinfulness and smallness on the other. It is a gap which cannot be breached by human presumption or initiative or comprehension. It is a gap unbridgeable by anything *we* do and is overcome only by what God does in our Lord Jesus Christ and which we receive from Him.

The Holy Father Benedict XVI has repeatedly warned against the tendency in modern times for liturgical prayer to drift toward a celebration of the community, and John Paul II insisted in a pointed analysis of elements undignified and inappropriate to liturgical prayer that "it is necessary to purify worship of deformations, of careless forms of expression, of ill-prepared music and texts which are not very suited to the grandeur of the Act being celebrated." In all the several liturgical rites and uses of the Church, then, we are in common urged to seek only those elements which authentically and worthily reflect the august sacrifice they embody.

Thus today in the ancient Roman Rite, we bow as did our fathers in the Faith, we kneel as those before us did many centuries ago, we prostrate ourselves before the awesome re-presentation on the altar of the Sacrifice of the Cross. The Epistle of today's feast reminds us that even at the name of Jesus, every knee should bow of those that are in heaven, on earth and under the

Sermon of Father Calvin Goodwin, FSSP

earth–the Church Militant, the Church Triumphant, and the Church Suffering. If this is the appropriate action to the *mention* of the Holy Name, how much more reverence and devotion should inform our acknowledgment of His actual Presence on the altar? Nothing casual, but instead a communal turning toward the Lord. Once again, the words of our Holy Father, "A turning to the Lord in gratitude, love and awe, for what is donated to us by a merciful God and which we could never achieve on our own or make happen for ourselves." And by this humble submission, we are united, as St. Paul reminds us, to the Church Triumphant in heaven and the Church Suffering in Purgatory, in offering to God our common homage.

The first thing that we have to understand, then, is that this Mystery takes us beyond the limits available to unaided human understanding. It cannot be grasped or encompassed by the puny human intellect alone, darkened as it is by the inroads of sin. We can find our way to it only through a humble, reverent, and faith-founded attentiveness. Not a passivity, mind you, but an attention which is in fact the activity most essential to our participation in Holy Mass. As Pope John Paul II put it, making his own the words of St. Augustine from so long ago but still wholly normative for all authentic Catholic worship, "The highest music is one that arises from our hearts." It is precisely this harmony that God wants to hear in our liturgies.

The most perfect participation in that Sacrifice is in fact exemplified by Our Blessed Lady at the foot of the Cross. And what is it that Our Lady does there at the foot of the Cross? Nothing in fact that mortal eyes can perceive. What does she say there at the foot of the Cross?

Sacred Then and Sacred Now

Nothing that mortal ears can hear. And yet no human being ever was or ever could be more fully or more intimately involved in that Sacrifice than she was at that moment, because her heart and soul and being were united to her Son and to what He was doing for us all. As always, she shows us the way.

Thus, with Our Lady at the foot of the Cross, we too can only be present and wonder, asking ourselves in union with the prayer of the priest at the altar, *Quid retribuam*: "What return shall I make to the Lord for all that He hath given unto me?" This is both the beginning and the goal of participation in the Holy Sacrifice of the Mass. Everything that fails to lead to that reverence and interior union, or which impedes it, impedes authentic participation, and all the elements of exterior participation consonant with these principles will inevitably have the character of authenticity. And when that Sacrifice is crowned in the moment of Holy Communion, what is it that we do? We receive. We receive what we could never fashion or make for ourselves, but which is freely and mercifully and lovingly given to us by a loving and merciful God in His Son, our Savior, the Body and Blood, Soul and Divinity of the Son of God, a moment above all for devout and humble receptivity.

This is the moment of Mount Tabor, when the apostles are rapt in silent wonder, their heads bowed low in awe and holy fear, until, as St. Matthew tells us, Jesus came and touched them and then, looking up, they saw only Jesus. That is a text in which the early Christians–and Christians of all time–will certainly have recognized their own rite of Holy Communion. Through this rite of Holy Mass, and not infrequently without particular verbal comprehension, saints and martyrs have

Sermon of Father Calvin Goodwin, FSSP

been raised up in the Church. Simple people and children have entered into heroic holiness, not because they grasped or saw, but because they revered and believed. How young people today need that simple and humble faith of a Thérèse of the Child Jesus, who said at the very end of her life, "I always sought only the Truth." How we need that simple and humble faith of a Bernadette, who attested, when questioned by the priest, that she did not understand the awesome message that Our Lady had chosen her to convey, but nevertheless her faith in Our Lady was real and wholly unshakable. And thus that faith became richly fruitful for her own relationship with God, as well as for the mission that had been entrusted to her.

Yet how many have forgotten that their first responsibility in this world is to know God through the exercise of the virtue of faith? The world's modalities are insufficient in themselves for divine worship. We must surrender to the Christ, our Light who alone guides us beyond the world's deceptions to the realm of divinely given revelation. And that revealed truth is made present here today and every day that Holy Mass is celebrated in all the approved rites of the Church through the renewal of the Sacrifice of the Cross.

Finally, let us be clear: no one here has the slightest intention of proposing the immemorial liturgy as some solution to the Church's trials or troubles. The purpose of liturgical prayer is, in any case, not to *fix* things in the Church but so to unite us to Christ our Lord that we can navigate the troubled sea of this world—always oriented towards, and one day finding our repose in, Him. But the Church will surely benefit so much from the reintegration into her life of this "most beautiful thing this side of

Sacred Then and Sacred Now

heaven," as Father Frederick Faber once memorably described the ancient rite of Holy Mass. Priests will benefit in their interior lives, and countless souls will benefit from that silence in which alone the voice of God may be discerned. No, this Mass is not a challenge to the Church, or an act of condemnation, or an act of politics, but an immeasurable enrichment of the Church's life. It is a sign of restoration, a sign of renewed vigor and self-awareness for and in the Church. We should familiarize ourselves with the provisions that the Holy Father has made in *Summorum Pontificum*, and ponder them for the wisdom they embody beyond their immediate practical prescriptions. The Sacrifice of the Cross in this ancient and venerable form is to be exalted, as is the Cross itself, in this ancient and venerable feast that we celebrate today.

About the Author

Thomas E. Woods, Jr., holds a bachelor's degree in history from Harvard and his master's, M. Phil., and Ph.D. from Columbia University. His other books include *33 Questions About American History You're Not Supposed to Ask*; the *New York Times* national bestseller *The Politically Incorrect Guide to American History*; *How the Catholic Church Built Western Civilization*; *The Church Confronts Modernity*; and *The Church and the Market: A Catholic Defense of the Free Economy* (first-place winner in the 2006 Templeton Enterprise Awards).

Woods' writing has appeared in dozens of popular and scholarly periodicals, including the *American Historical Review*, the *Christian Science Monitor*, *Investor's Business Daily*, *Catholic Historical Review*, *Modern Age*, *American Studies*, *Catholic Social Science Review*, *Inside the Vatican*, *University Bookman*, *Journal of Markets & Morality*, *New Oxford Review*, *Catholic World Report*, *Independent Review*, *Religion & Liberty*, *Journal des Economistes et des Etudes Humaines*, *AD2000* (Australia), *Christian Order* (U.K.), *Crisis*, and *Human Rights Review*.

Woods is the host of a television series for EWTN called "The Catholic Church: Builder of Civilization." He lives in Alabama with his wife and family, and maintains a website at ThomasEWoods.com.